Jump In

Teacher's Guide

2nd Edition

ISBN 13: 9781090531315

Jump In

Teacher's Guide

Middle School Composition

2nd Edition

Sharon Watson

Table of Contents

Schedules

Jump In, 2nd Edition covers a four-year range of middle school grades and writing abilities. For that reason, we've included a variety of useful schedules to help your composition class fit your students and your plans. As you can see, you have a great deal of flexibility here.

One-year plan

If you have only one year to use *Jump In, 2nd Edition*, we recommend completing these chapters:

"Get Your Feet Wet"
"Opinions—You've Got Them"
"Persuasion: The Basics"
"A How-to"
"A Report"
"Compare and Contrast"
Skill 1: Your Own Story from "Narration" *Pg 225*

Dip into the 10-Minute Writing Plunges program during the year (page 41). *M T W Th*

Two-year plan

If you would like to stroll through *Jump In, 2nd Edition* at a more leisurely pace, feel free to use the following plan:

up+ Pg 249

Complete "Get Your Feet Wet" through "A Report" in the first year. In the second year, finish "A Biography" through "Poetry."

When students get to the essay assignment at the end of each chapter, put the textbook aside as they work through the assignment, suggested writing schedule, and the accompanying checklist. That way, students can concentrate on their current essay assignment without being bogged down with new information from the next chapter.

When the essay is completed on time, move to the next chapter.

This pace also gives you time to repeat a lesson or section if you see that your student does not understand the material or could use more practice in it.

Dip into the 10-Minute Writing Plunges program during the year (page 41).

Three-year plan

If you have a young, reluctant, or inexperienced writer, you may want to use the three-year plan:

Begin the year with a few weeks of the 10-Minute Writing Plunges, *Jump In*'s writing prompts program (page 41).

Complete a chapter in *Jump In, 2ⁿᵈ Edition* and then use a week or two of the 10-Minute Writing Plunges again.

Continue alternating between chapters and Plunges.

When students get to the essay assignment at the end of each chapter, put the textbook aside as they work through the assignment, suggested writing schedule, and the accompanying checklist. That way, students can concentrate on their current essay assignment without being bogged down with new information from the next chapter.

When the essay is completed on time, take a break from the textbook and do a few writing prompts from the 10-Minute Writing Plunges program (page 41).

Random Facts

- *Jump In, 2nd Edition* contains 98 daily lessons called Skills, with an additional 19 Skills that are the assignments and checklists.
- Each daily lesson will take anywhere from five to twenty minutes to complete.
- Students learn how to write paragraphs, different types of paragraphs, topic sentences, and main ideas (thesis statements), with reinforcement throughout the year.
- They also learn how to write nine types of essays and one research report, complete with lessons on in-text citations and citing their sources.
- Proofreading lessons are included.
- Students evaluate other students' essays in the textbook. This way, they can see what an essay in their age group looks like, and they can apply what they see in the example essay to their own writing.
- Copious examples abound in the textbook.
- Moments of humor may pop up randomly at any time in the lessons.
- Experienced writers have different word counts for their essays and some exclusive lessons.
- Students will learn two solid methods of compare-and-contrast writing.
- You will need a separate grammar course. However, the following proofreading and grammar tutorials are available at Writing with Sharon Watson:

https://writingwithsharonwatson.com/grammar-tutorials-bundle/
https://writingwithsharonwatson.com/proofreading-tutorials-bundle/
https://writingwithsharonwatson.com/estore/grammar-lets-eat-ebook/

- Each essay assignment now comes with a suggested writing schedule and a checklist in the textbook.
- Check at the end of each day to see if your student has completed that day's task in the checklist. That way, the essay isn't one huge assignment; it is a series of small, achievable steps.
- Teachers have detailed and specific grading grids for each essay assignment to make grading easier. Find the grids in the section labeled Grading Grids.

The Assignments

Opinions—You've Got Them
Write an opinion essay.
Word count: at least 150 words. Experienced writers: at least 200 words.

Persuasion: The Basics
Write a persuasive essay.
Word count: at least 200 words. Experienced writers: 250 words.

Cause and Effect
Write a cause-and-effect persuasive essay.
Word count: at least 250 words. Experienced writers: at least 300 words.

A Newspaper Article
Write a newspaper article.
Word count: 200-300 words.

A How-to
Write a how-to in the essay method (300-500 words) or the instruction-manual method (150-300 words).

A Report
Write a research report.
New writers: at least 400 words. Experienced writers: at least 500 words.

A Biography
Write a biography.
Word count: at least 300 words. Experienced writers: at least 350 words.

Compare and Contrast
New writers: Write a compare-and-contrast paragraph in the block method.
Word count: approximately 100 words.

Experienced writers: Write a compare-and-contrast essay in the feature method.
Word count: at least 350 words.

A Book Report
Write a book report using the Book Report Form.
Word count: at least 300 words. Experienced writers: at least 350 words.

A Book Response
Complete an artistic-skill book response or a writing-skill book response.

Description
Rewrite a boring paragraph to make it sparkle.
Describe a room.
Describe a person or character.
Describe a scene.
Create a mood.

Narration
Write a personal narrative. Word count: at least 300.
Write story hooks.
Write a scene to reveal a character trait. Word count: at least 250 words.
Write a story in first or third-person point of view. Word count: at least 250 words.
Write a story from a scenario to resolve a conflict. Word count: at least 300 words.
Write a scene with dialog and narrative actions. Word count: at least 200 words.
Write a fairy tale, tall tale, Just So story, or parable.

Poetry
Write a haiku.
Write a cinquain.
Write a diamante.
Write a limerick.
Write a hymn.
Imitate a poem.
Write new lyrics to a song.

The Teacher's Backpack

Helpful tools such as Mistake Medic and Create Your Own Paragraph

Table of contents for the student textbook

Mistake Medic

1. Reread your paper to check the **content and expression of ideas**:
   - Does it have an interesting title?
   - Does the opening sentence or paragraph grab the reader's attention by stating a fact, using a quotation, telling a story, or asking a question?
   - Is the main idea/thesis statement clear?
   - Does the paper support it well?
   - Does your paper get to the point quickly?
   - Does it stick to the point?
   - Are the points or reasons solid?
   - Do the paragraphs support each topic sentence well?
   - Is there a logical progression from one point to the next?
   - Is it easy to read and easy to understand?
   - Does the conclusion give the reader something interesting to think about?

Then read for **grammar and the mechanics** of writing:

2. Check your title for correct capital letters. Don't underline it or put quotation marks around it. Skip a line after the title.
3. Is your paper double-spaced?
4. Did you indent (five spaces) the first line of every paragraph?
5. Read your paper aloud. Is anything confusing? Add words or change them as necessary.
6. Look for unnecessarily repeated words. Use specific adjectives and nouns and powerful verbs. But don't get fancy.
7. Read your paper out loud to find run-on sentences and sentence fragments.
8. Make sure all of your commas are there for a reason, not just because you want to pause or have to hiccup. Check your other punctuation. Refer to a grammar book.
9. Check your capital letters. Every sentence begins with one. Proper nouns need one.
10. Circle possible spelling mistakes and homonym mistakes (*there, their,* and *they're,* for example). Then look them up in a dictionary.
11. Try these **tricks** to catch more mistakes. You'll be surprised how many more you find:
    a. **Print your paper** instead of proofreading it at the computer screen.
    b. **Resize the font** or choose another font. This moves the words into new positions, making it easier to catch mistakes you normally would read over.
    c. **Read your paper out loud** and listen to what you are saying.
    d. **Read each word.** Don't skim.

Tips to Help Your Student Proofread

These are choices, not a chronological list (apologies for the consistent "he"):

☐ Tell him to **print out each version** as he edits it, showing you the progression of his proofreading.

☐ Tell him to **double-space** his work and **print it off**. He will find many more mistakes and ideas for revisions this way and will have room to correct them.

☐ Listen to your student **read the paper out loud.** The number of mistakes he finds this way will surprise both of you. He should have his pen handy for this exercise.

☐ Ask to see the **outline, list, cluster, Greek temple, or sticky notes** he used to organize his thoughts. This makes him aware of his need to organize before he writes.

☐ Ask what his **topic** is. Also ask for his **main idea** or **thesis statement** for the whole paper. He should be able to sum it up in 20 words or less.

☐ Ask him what the **topic sentence** is for each paragraph.

☐ Ask if the **order of his points** is the best one for his readers.

☐ Put a **check mark** next to any line that has a mistake. Then he can look for the mistake.

☐ Put a check mark next to any line that has a mistake and **label the mistake:** comma, question mark, missing a word or two, run-on sentence, sentence fragment, and so on. Then he can look for it.

☐ Circle the **spelling mistakes** but don't correct them. Consider including some of your student's common spelling mistakes on the next spelling test.

☐ At the bottom of the page, write **how many grammar and/or punctuation mistakes you found.** Then help your student find them.

☐ Review Mistake Medic on the previous page with him. He should use this for every assignment. His copy is in My Locker at the end of *Jump In, 2nd Edition*.

Use these handy tutorials:
https://writingwithsharonwatson.com/grammar-tutorials-bundle/
https://writingwithsharonwatson.com/proofreading-tutorials-bundle/
https://writingwithsharonwatson.com/estore/grammar-lets-eat-ebook/

The Steps of Writing

(Your students have this information in My Locker at the end of their textbook.)

Brainstorm. Write down ideas. If your teacher lets you choose the topic, list things you know a lot about or are interested in. If your teacher chooses a large subject, list smaller topics inside this subject.

Narrow down your ideas. You can't possibly use all of your ideas in your assignment. Keep the ones you can use and cross out the rest. Sometimes you won't know which ones to keep until you begin to research or write.

Organize your ideas. Use a list, outline, cluster, Greek temple, or sticky notes to organize all the ideas you intend to keep.

Choose an effective point order. Arrange your points into an order that makes sense to you and your readers.

Begin writing. Use the list you just made. Begin at any point in your essay (body, intro, or conclusion). Put each point in its own paragraph. Forget about mistakes. Write now; fix later. This is your first draft. Some call it a rough draft or a sloppy copy. <u>Never</u> hand a first draft to your teacher as the finished assignment.

Let your paper rest. Set it aside for a few hours or days. This means you won't be able to wait until the last minute to write it. When you set it aside, you are giving it time to cool off so that you can do the next two steps with a level head.

Read your paper out loud. Do the ideas flow well from one point to the next? Are you saying what you really want to say? Have you expressed the ideas as best you can?

Proofread it. Comb through your paper. Use the numerous checklists after each assignment and refer to the Mistake Medic. Look for all sorts of mistakes, one sentence at a time.

Write or type the final draft. Make it as polished and as neat as possible. Double-spaced, too. Before handing it in, read it one more time out loud— slowly—to look for mistakes.

Hand it in on time. If you have done all these steps well, both you and your teacher will be proud of your work.

Why a Reluctant Writer Hates to Write

(and What You Can Do About It)

1. He received negative feedback in earlier grades that discouraged him.

Evaluate his work objectively by using the grading grids that begin on page 91. Point out what he does well. Layer on the encouragement. Writing is not easy.

2. His strengths lie elsewhere: math, science, working with his hands, sports, relationships, music, and so forth.

Tap into his strengths and interests. He can write his opinion on why everyone should be smart in math. Tie writing to science by assigning him a short report on a topic of interest to him. A kinesthetic student can write a how-to on something he knows how to do. Your sports lover can write a play-by-play of an exciting part of a game or write how to play a sport. A relationship-oriented student can write with a friend, write an advice column, or compose essays on friendship or the perils of gossiping. A musician can describe what it feels like to play music.

3. She believes that writing is a secret art with no discernable rules into which she must enter with a secret password that she doesn't have.

Your student will learn very specific patterns and formats in *Jump In, 2nd Edition*. Review Mistake Medic in the textbook's My Locker with her.

4. She doesn't have enough time to think about and write her assignments.

Allow her enough time to perform these separate operations: brainstorming, writing, and proofreading. Help her use the suggested writing schedule for each assignment. Allow at least one hour for every 100 words assigned.

5. He is a perfectionist who forces himself to have everything in order (including his thoughts) before he will write.

In *Jump In, 2nd Edition*, he will learn how to brainstorm. Brainstorm with him on fun topics without making him write the accompanying essay. He then will make lists of ideas or points *on paper* so he can arrange them later in an effective order. Immerse him in the 10-Minute Writing Plunges (page 41), which will allow him to write without being graded on everything he writes.

6. Earlier writing assignments were too difficult for him, so he gave up.

Encourage him. Find something he did well and tell him so. Use the incremental lessons and low word counts in *Jump In, 2nd Edition*. Ask him what is hard about writing and help him find the answers in this book or in his grammar book.

Create Your Own Paragraph

What's your topic?

What's the main idea (the one point you want to make in this paragraph)?

List three statements, facts, or examples that answer "Why?" or "Prove it!"

1.

Transition needed?

2.

Transition needed?

3.

Do you need any transitions like *otherwise, however, in addition, for example, furthermore, afterward,* or *finally* between your three statements? Write them next to "Transition needed?"

Do you need a sentence at the end of your paragraph to sum up your idea or move readers from this paragraph to the next one? If so, write it here:

(You have permission to copy this page as often as needed for constructing your paragraphs.)

Opinions and Persuasion—What to Look For

Writing an opinion

1. What is the topic? What is the student's opinion on the topic? These should be clear and appear in the first paragraph. (Simple examples: "I'm against the war in Reykjavik" or "Candy bars make great snacks.")

2. Is the first sentence interesting enough that the reader wants to keep reading?

3. Does each following paragraph (except for the conclusion) tell a new reason why your student is for the idea or against it? One reason = one paragraph.

4. In what order are the reasons/paragraphs? They should be in an effective order for the readers.

5. Does the last paragraph (the conclusion) restate the student's opinion in a different form, giving the reader something to think about?

6. Has your student written the opinion without making fun of those who believe differently?

Writing to persuade

Add the following to the above list. After brainstorming ideas, the student should write a purpose statement to guide him: "I am going to convince the reader that...." This sentence will not appear in the essay.

1. Has the student considered the audience? Writing to peers will be different than writing to the local newspaper or the church newsletter.

2. Does the introductory paragraph begin with an interesting statement, fact, or quotation, a story to illustrate the point, or a pointed question to make the reader think? Does the conclusion give food for thought and include a call to action?

3. Has the student shown he knows both sides of the argument by respectfully mentioning an opposing view and refuting it? ("Some say..., but scientists have shown that....")

4. Has the student included not just opinions but facts to back up those opinions?

5. Are all the points aimed at persuading readers?

6. Has the student correctly cited his sources?

DON'T List for Persuasion

(Students have this list in "Persuasion: The Basics," Skill 10.)

1. **Don't insult** a person or an entire group.

Example: Did you kids even look at yourselves in the mirror before you left the house? You're a mess!

2. **Don't wander** off your subject.

Example: I hope the library buys *Out of the Dust* by Karen Hesse. I read a lot of books. Just last week I read two books by Frank Peretti. He sure is a good writer. I want to read more by him.

3. **Don't contradict** yourself.

Example: The team sure could use me at first base. That's my strongest position unless I'm playing shortstop.

4. **Don't go on and on.** Keep it short and sweet.

Example: Putting a statue in the middle of our park was so stupid. I mean, who needs another statue? We already have four around town. Why do we need one more bronze hero up on a horse? Our town will get a bad reputation for all the statues we have cluttering up the landscape, and no one knows who those guys are anymore. There's one on the square, one at the post office, one at the school, one prancing on the hill, and now this one at the park. It's too much.

5. **Don't use "I think...," "I believe...," or "It is my opinion that...."**

No: It is my opinion that students should eat a chocolate bar every day.

Yes: Students should eat a chocolate bar every day.

6. **Don't write without evidence**; don't exclude facts.

Example: Probably some other towns have recycling bins, too. I can't think of any right now, but I'm sure there are some.

7. **Don't be vague.**

Example: I want to talk to you about a problem in our town. It has been here for a long time. Everyone is bothered by it. Can't you see how bad it has gotten in the past year? Isn't it awful? And now it's time to do something about it.

8. **Don't be illogical**; don't draw the wrong conclusions.

Example: No one waited on me, even though I was there first. I know it was because of my red hair and freckles. The employees must hate red hair and freckles. They waited on two blondes before they would even look at me.

9. **Don't use jargon** (lingo) or technical words that only a few know unless you define them right away.

Example: Be sure to attach the widget to the doohickey just under the spanner.

10. **Don't threaten** your audience or yell at them.

Example: If I were you, I would watch out from now on! The next time I go into your red-hair-and-freckles-hating store, I'm going to do some damage! You'll see. You can't ignore me and get away with it.

> Avoid everything on the DON'T LIST. Using anything from that list will only weaken your argument and make you look like you don't know what you're doing.

DO List for Persuasion

(Students have this list in "Persuasion: The Basics," Skill 10.)

1. **Do treat** your reader intelligently.

Yes: Teens, please show that you respect yourselves by dressing modestly.

2. **Do talk fairly** about the opposing view. Then prove it incorrect (refute it).

Yes: Many women say that abortion is an important part of women's rights. They want to be able to make decisions for themselves about their bodies. And that seems logical until you realize that there are a lot of little baby girls who will never have any rights because someone made the decision of death for them.

3. **Do quote** people, experts, or the Bible.

Yes: I'm the right person for the first base position. Even Coach McGraw said last year, "If you want first base done right, rely on Pat. Nobody's better."

4. **Do be clear** about what you're talking about.

Yes: When I finished reading *Out of the Dust*, I knew other teens would like it. That's why I hope the library buys it.

5. **Do identify yourself** if it adds to your topic.

Yes: I am a frequent babysitter, so I know the importance of first-aid training.

6. **Do define** your terms.

Yes: Open your bumbershoot (umbrella) with care.

7. **Do know your audience.** Know their age, gender, interests, and so forth.

No for a newspaper: Various personages subscribe to the fortuitous vicissitudes of existence. [This means that some people believe in chance, but it is too wordy for a newspaper, which is normally written for a 12-year-old reading level.]

Yes: When you give your testimony in church, you use words and phrases that everyone there understands. But when you talk to a friend who is not a Christian and who hasn't ever been to church, you will use words that he understands. You will mean the same thing, but you will use different words.

> Use everything from the **DO LIST** that will help your paper. You will strengthen your argument and sound more intelligent.

Different Ways to Write Biographies

Students have this list in "A Biography," Skill 2.

1. Write about a person's accomplishments: If he hadn't been born, then we wouldn't have _____ or we wouldn't know _____.

2. Write about the part of his childhood that is the key to his future accomplishments.

3. Write about the life of someone you respect. Use her accomplishments and difficulties to show why you respect her.

4. Write about the life of someone you don't respect. Choose a person from history or a person in the public eye today. Write about his negative accomplishments or character flaws to show why you don't respect him.

5. Write a "Who Am I?" in which you tell interesting things about the person but save the name for near the end of your biography.

6. Write about an important or pivotal day in the life of your person. Show what happened and how it changed him or her.

7. Write about a person's spiritual development throughout his or her life.

8. Write an imaginary page from your person's journal, diary, or letter. Show the reader what your person was like. Include facts.

Book Report Form

PARAGRAPH 1:

Title of book: _____

Type of book (genre): _____

Year it was first published: _____

Author: _____

(Form continues on next page.)

PARAGRAPHS 1 AND 2:

Setting. Identify the time and place:

Main characters. Label one or two protagonists and one antagonist and then give a short description of each; include page numbers:

1.

2.

3.

Conflicts. List the main character's two biggest problems:

1.

2.

(Form continues on next page)

PARAGRAPH 2, continued:

Plot. The story begins when . . .

The story gets bad when . . .

The story is the very worst—and the main character has to make a major decision—when . . .

The story wraps up when . . .

Sum up the plot (action—what the character *does*) in 40 words or less:

(Form continues on next page.)

PARAGRAPH 3:

Theme. What idea about life does the author say through this book? List examples and page numbers where you find examples of this:

Short author biography. (Any biographical information that relates to the theme will go in this paragraph.)

PARAGRAPH 4:

Special features. Note great descriptions, plot twists, similes, symbols, surprises, and so on. Use examples and page numbers:

(Form continues on next page.)

My opinions

Something that makes the book powerful or interesting:

Something that makes the book weak or boring:

The character I most strongly identified with is

because

What I learned from this book or what impact it had on me:

I ☐ liked   ☐ didn't like   this book because ⟹

How was reading the book different from what I expected it would be?

(End of form)

A Book Response

Students have this list in "A Book Response," Skill 1.

Artistic Skills

1. **Draw, paint, or sculpt** an interesting character or exciting scene from the book. Label the work or include a caption.

2. **Create a mural** with friends. Illustrate a setting or a scene.

3. Make a **3-D scene** in a box (a diorama) or create a scene with LEGOs® to illustrate a section of the story. Use the author's description of that scene. Try to capture the mood, too.

4. **Draw a map** for the inside cover of the book, labeling the lands and landmarks where characters traveled. If it is a journey, show the beginning and the destination. Include the dangerous places. Color your map if you want to.

5. Research the kinds of clothing, weapons, dwellings, vehicles, or furniture the characters in your story might have used. **Draw or paint** pictures of them, **build** a model or replica, or **sew** the clothes.

6. **Act out** an important scene from the book with a friend or two in front of an audience. Use costumes and props.

Writing Skills

7. Make a **report card** for the author. Grade him or her on the basics: setting, characters, plot, and so forth. Also give a grade on how the author begins and ends the book, if the book held your attention, if the author uses special features like similes and metaphors, and so on. Include why you gave the author those grades and what he or she can do to improve.

8. Write a **story or poem** of your own based on something you read in the book.

9. Write a **letter to the author**. Ask her something about the book or tell her something. If the author is still living, send your letter to the publisher listed on the inside of your book. You may get a letter in return!

10. Write a letter to an **imaginary librarian** telling her why she should buy this book for the library. Tell her a little bit about the book, why it will appeal to other readers, and why you liked it.

11. Write a **blurb** (the part of the story you find on the back cover of the book). Tell enough of the story to get the reader interested—but don't tell the ending!

12. Write a pretend **phone conversation** or **text exchange** between you and a friend. Tell her why you think she would like the story and what you liked about it. Or tell her *not* to read it and what you *didn't* like about it.

13. Read about any **animals** in the book and write a short report or give a short speech on them. Or write a short story with them in it.

14. Write a **negative blurb** for the back of the book, telling readers why they *shouldn't* read the book. This is usually a humorous blurb that has the opposite effect on readers. It actually encourages them to read the book.

15. Write a TV or radio **commercial** for the book.

Sample Essay Evaluations

Example essays to show how to earn an A, B, C, D, or F

How Do I Give a Grade?

Read the assignment for **content** first. Did the student follow the directions? Is the paper clear? Is it in a logical order? Are the ideas expressed well? Is the thesis statement well supported? These questions and others are clearly delineated in each grading grid here in the teacher's guide. Grading grids begin on page 91.

Next, read it for **grammar and mechanics**. Punctuation, capitalization, spelling, paragraphing, and good grammar go in this category. At these grade levels, we recommend that you <u>do not correct everything that is wrong.</u> A young writer tends to dry up and stop writing if he is graded on everything he writes all the time. (Think of a new bride being evaluated by her husband on all of her cooking.) Consider choosing a particular focus each month or semester—commas, spelling, and so on—and grade that.

Give two grades for each assignment: one for the content and one for the grammar and mechanics. For the same assignment, the grades often are quite different from one another.

Use the specific grading grids for each essay assignment. All grading grids are included in this Teacher's Guide in the section labeled Grading Grids.

Peruse the **sample evaluations** on the following pages. I haven't corrected everything that was wrong on those papers. My aim was to instruct and encourage my students. Be judicious about what you correct or mention to your student. Your student's papers will not be perfect.

For every item you mention for improvement, mention one or two that the student is doing well.

Don't aim for perfection; aim for progress.

Above all, **be encouraging.**

How to Earn an A

Grading papers can be tricky and—yes—sometimes even subjective. By using the specific and objective grading grids found in the Grading Grids section of this Teacher's Guide, you can smooth some of the subjectivity out of your grading and give a fair grade. These forms also take some of the burden off you and put it squarely where it should be—on the student!

Below is a biography written by a fifth-grade girl who definitely earned an A. It appears in its original form. Read this 491-word paper and the following comments to find out what makes this an A paper.

A Cellist of Conscience

"I will tell you what I will do to him if I catch him. I will cut off his arms both of them at the elbows." This was the threat made by General Gonzalo Queipo de Llano to Pablo over the radio in 1936. His threats were dismissed and Pablo continued his stand against the Spanish Fascists.

Pablo was a small man in stature, born to Carlos and Pilar of Catalonia, Spain in 1876. Even though Carlos was a great conductor and led the local church choir, he did not want his son to grow up to be a musician. He knew that he could not earn enough money to support a family; only the best of the best could obtain wealth. However, for Pablo, musical notes were as familiar as words. He studied the piano with his father and by the age of six was playing simpler pieces of Beethoven, Mendelssohn, Chopin, and Bach. He longed to learn how to play the organ, but his father would not let him begin until his feet could reach the pedals. This took longer than most children because Pablo in adulthood only stood five feet and three inches tall.

Later, in 1885 a band of traveling musicians came through town. Pablo became fascinated by an instrument he had never seen before. It was made with a broom handle and strung like a cello, although he had never seen or heard of a cello before. He ran home and told his father that he wanted one. Carlos and Pilar were very poor. Therefore, Carlos agreed to make an instrument like the one he had seen. They made it from a long slender gourd and after a few minutes of playing it, he played a tune by Schubert. Immediately, he fell in love with this homemade instrument. It was not until he was eleven that he first heard a real cello being played. He then longed to learn how to play it. He began holding his violin like a cello between his legs instead of tucked under his chin. His father was outraged, but his mother insisted that he have the chance to study the cello.

Pablo eventually obtained a cello. When he was seventeen years old he played for the Queen of Madrid and in 1896 he played at the royal palace in Portugal. He was awarded a grant to study the cello at the Madrid Conservatory of Music. He soon became the greatest cellist in the world. He used to play his cello for political reasons. For many decades he refused to play his cello publicly for any government that supported the Fascist government of Spain. He eventually had to live in exile in Puerto Rico. In 1971 Pablo composed and performed a hymn for the United Nations.

Pablo Casals, called Pau, meaning peace, suffered from a heart attack in 1973 and died. He will always be remembered as the "Cellist of Conscience."

CONTENT:

This gal does everything right. She begins with an interesting quotation that pulls the reader into the biography. She tells the story of Pablo Casals in a clear, chronological way, beginning with his early life, continuing through to the genesis of his love of the cello, and on to his fame and political life. The reader can feel the longing Pablo must have felt as he watched his poor father craft a musical instrument for him to play. It is clear that Pablo developed not only musical talents but political convictions as well. The student ties the end to the beginning by writing about Pablo's convictions in both.

An older student would have developed the theme of Pablo's political conscience, including the people and events that shaped his views. However, for a fifth-grade paper, this student's work is admirable.

GRAMMAR/MECHANICS:

There is an introduction and conclusion. Each paragraph contains specific information about Pablo in a chronological way, stepping from paragraph to paragraph as the musician grows older.

There are a few comma mistakes that are quite normal for a fifth-grade student. For example, here are some corrections:

- "I will cut off his arms, both of them, at the elbows."
- ...born to Carlos and Pilar of Catalonia, Spain, in 1876.
- ...he played for the queen of Madrid, and in 1896 he played at the royal palace in Portugal.

This student uses implied topic sentences. For instance, the subject of paragraph three is definitely how Pablo's love of the cello began. She uses the transition words *later* and *eventually* in paragraphs three and four to move the topic forward.

This paper earned an *A* in content and an *A* in Grammar/mechanics.

How to Earn a B

A girl in the eighth grade wrote this 760-word report on volcanoes. Please read her paper below in its original form and the discussion of her grade that follows.

Volcanoes

There have been many terrible volcanoes in this world, and seeing as volcanoes are what this report is about, I'll share a few with you now. This is not a complete list, it's just some of the majors.

At 8:30 am, May 18, 1980, Mount St. Helens in Washington erupted. Seismographic activity was recorded 20 miles north of Mount St. Helens by the University of Washington in Seattle on March 20th. This activity increased until March 27th, when she blew ash and vapor 20,000 feet into the air leaving a crater 250 feet in diameter. Two days later, on the 29th, another cloud of this sort reached as far south as Bend, Oregon, 150 miles south of Mount St. Helens. But, wait, I'm not done! After this, a bulge developed on the south side of the mountain that was 2,000 feet long and 500 feet high. Now, before I tell you what happened to this bulge, I have to say that this volcano was of a great help to expand our knowledge of volcanoes. Okay, back to this bulge. Well, it exploded on May 18, 1980, blowing ash 12 miles into the air. The impact knocked 150 square miles of trees down that were 20 miles away. When it blew, there was a landslide that displaced one river into another causing flooding. All and all, more than 100 people were dead or missing and there was $1.5 billion or more in total damage.

Another great volcano was in 79 A.D. when the mountain of Vesivius, Italy, destroyed Pompeii and Herculaneum. Ash rained down and it was as dark as night. Herculaneum was covered by mudflows while Pompeii was lost to ash and sulfur. The most interesting thing about Vesivius was that the townspeople got frozen in time. The ash and mud preserved the town perfectly. There were saloons with liquor stains on the counters and kitchens with pans and food still there. Almost everything was still intact.

April 5, 1815. It was thought to be extinct. Tambor, near Java, Indonesia, was 12,000 feet high. When it exploded, an unusual amount of ash went up into the atmosphere, changing the global climate. 1815 was called "the year with no summer." The winter wasn't bitter, but some inches of snow were reported in New England in June. Although, in New England there are many things that grow well and even thrive in the colder weather. This prompted Canada to buy some of our food, which, in turn, made grain prices soar. And in poor France political turmoil reigned, where they had just finished with the

Napoleonic War. But back to the volcano. This large cloud darkened the sky for 300 miles away. The eruptions weren't over 'til July (at which April 11-12 were the strongest). The site of the village of Tambora was covered with 18 feet of water and 12,000 natives died. In the end, the mountain of Tambora stood nearly one mile shorter than it was.

Arguably, this next one is the most well-known volcano in history. Krakatoa, Sunda Strait, Indonesia, August 26-27, 1883. Gases had built up inside Krakatoa. The island of Krakatoa destroyed itself. On the 27th explosions were heard from 5:30 am to 11:00 am from 3,000 miles away. Explosions that sent rocks flying into the air. The northern half of Krakatoa was completely gone and the explosions split Rakata from base to summit. This sent tsunamis that were reported to be 120 feet high ashore. Tens of thousands died from these tidal waves. The ash and vapor stayed in the atmosphere from the 1880's into the 1890's lowering the average temperature one degree Fahrenheit. These particles prompted a "green sun" in India. From the original island, Krakatoa, there's now Anak Krakatoa, Rakata, Pajanga and Sertung.

Another notable is Mount Pelee, Martinique. This explosion on May 8, 1902, wiped out the city of St. Pierre and killed more than 30,000 people with only six survivors, total. One of whom was a murderer named Joseph Surtout. He was locked away so far under that he was okay when they got him out four days later. This volcano was strange because there was no lava, only ashes, dust, gas and mud. Which was so thick, in fact, that when people called to each other, they could hear their own echoes.

As I said before, this list is far from complete. These volcanoes, along with many others, have impacted our lives heavily. But with every volcano eruption, comes more information about how to prepare and protect ourselves form future volcanoes.

CONTENT:

This student has done a lot of research on her subject, and she includes many interesting facts and stories. This is commendable. She also puts the volcanoes into a logical order: most famous in recent history, then back to AD 79, 1815, 1883, and 1902 (in ascending order from history). Each volcano resides in its own paragraph. The student includes an introductory and a concluding paragraph. It is clear that she uses some organizational and note-taking skills.

She earned a B this way: Other than recounting famous volcanoes, her paper lacks a unifying theme. She mentions how studying volcanoes "was of a great help to expand our knowledge" of them, that volcanoes "have impacted our lives heavily," and that we now have "more information about how to prepare and protect ourselves from future volcanoes." Any of these would be excellent themes to develop in her paper, but she fails to expand on any of them.

Her introduction does not begin with an interesting story, statement, fact, quotation, or question. It also does not guide the reader into the body. Her conclusion includes some themes that are new to the paper, either of which would have been usable for the whole paper. The conclusion is not the place to introduce something new to the paper but should tie the end to the beginning, challenge the reader, or give the reader something to think about.

By the time a student reaches junior high, she should be able to choose a main idea and develop it throughout the paper. Her thesis statement should be clear and appear somewhere near the end of the first paragraph. In her head or in her notes, she should identify her main idea by stating, "In my paper, I want to say *this* about volcanoes." If she cannot identify her main idea in this way, she needs to back up and make some decisions about her topic, determining what she wants to say about it.

This student's tone (the attitude she brings to the subject) is too casual for a school paper. However, she has an easy writing style and usually tells a clear story. In paragraphs two and four, she moves off her stories but comes back to them quickly. If she had determined a unifying theme beforehand, she might not have gotten lost in those paragraphs.

GRAMMAR/MECHANICS:

On the whole, this is a fairly average eighth-grade paper. She uses commas correctly in dates and in places, usually. There are a few other places that could have used some commas, especially to aid in clarity. She includes an apostrophe in her dates to indicate the decade: 1880's. It is now currently acceptable to write dates without the apostrophe: 1880s.

Instead of a comma in the last sentence of paragraph one, a semicolon should be used. It is one way of connecting two complete sentences.

Times of day use periods, as a.m. or p.m. Years are labeled as AD 79 or 35 BC. The word *'til* should be written as *until* or *till*.

She misspells Vesuvius continually. In paragraph four, the reader has to guess whether the place name is Tambor or Tambora, as the writer uses both. Her third from the last word should be *from*, not *form*, something only careful reading will catch.

In paragraph four, she uses an acceptable sentence fragment: "But back to the volcano." However, in paragraphs five and six, she uses three unacceptable fragments: "Explosions that sent rocks flying into the air," "One of whom was a murderer named Joseph Surtout," and "Which was so thick, in fact, that when people called to each other, they could hear their own echoes."

This paper earned a *B* in content and a *B+* in grammar/mechanics.

How to Earn a C

Below is a persuasive paper written by a boy in the seventh grade. A persuasive paper aims at convincing the reader to think differently about a subject and to do something constructive in response (believe and behave a certain way).

Though he received only a C on this paper, some of his other work is so good that it is included in the student textbook as an example of how to do something well.

Please read the following assignment, which is as he wrote it, and then read what this fellow did right and where he can improve.

Conserve Natural Resources

I believe we need to conserve natural resources and I am going to state my opinion as well as other peoples opinions.

Many people do not believe it is necessary to conserve, because they mistakenly believe recources will last forever. Others know they need to conserve but do not care, because recources will not run out in their lifetime. The third group of people care and conserve resources.

Conservationists divide resources into four groups (1) inexhaustible resources such as sunlight and water (2) renewable resources like plants and animals (3) nonrenewable resources; most minerals fall into this category and (4) recycable resources some minerals and plastic go in this group.

There are many ways YOU can help save the environment. You can take newspapers and glass as well as plastic bottles to recycling centers. You can stop forests and jungles from being cut down, and many other ways.

Conservation is important to maintain the quality of life wich means to keep the environment healthy.

CONTENT:

This young writer does a few things well. His title is clear and to the point. He mentions that some people do not take conservation seriously—a view opposite to his. He educates the reader about the categories of natural resources, which indicates some level of research. He also suggests a few things the reader can do to help the environment. His last sentence contains what might be his thesis statement (main idea). He has an introductory paragraph, three paragraphs for a body, and a concluding paragraph—a good format to use.

The obvious question that comes to mind is this: Did he use an outline or organize his thoughts before he wrote? It is unlikely that he did. While he talks about the issue from many angles, he does not focus on one area or lead the reader from point to point in any logical progression. He mentions an opposing view but does not refute it. He does not develop the idea of four kinds of natural resources and what the reader can do about each one. In listing ways the reader could respond, he omits how the reader can "stop forests and jungles from being cut down."

His introduction does not begin with an interesting statement, fact, question, quotation, or story. He uses "I believe…" This is on the Don't List for persuasive writing, which students have in their textbooks. The introduction states what he is going to tell the reader instead of engaging the reader in the topic. The thesis statement belongs at the end of his first paragraph, not at the end of his paper.

His conclusion should use something that refers to his clever statement, fact, question, quotation, or story (which he omitted) in the introduction, and it should contain a call to action (which was in his fourth paragraph).

His persuasive paper reads more like a simple report on conservation that I would expect from the average fifth grader who did not take the time to think about what he wanted to convey to readers and then organize his thoughts before he wrote.

Because this paper was this student's first try at persuasion, it was important to encourage him instead of list all his deficiencies. Comments included what he did well and how his paper could be stronger (use an outline, focus on one element of conservation, refute opposite view points, and so forth). There's no sense in shooting down the bird you're trying to teach how to fly.

GRAMMAR/MECHANICS:

Words directly related to the topic should be spelled correctly. *Resources* is misspelled twice, *recyclable* once. His grade is slightly lower (C instead of B-) because he misspelled words that are important to his topic.

Peoples (paragraph one) should be *people's*. *Wich* (paragraph five) should be *which*.

This writer does a brave thing in his list in paragraph three. He uses a numerical method of listing, even though he does not punctuate it correctly. This is one correct way of fixing it:

> Conservationists divide resources into four groups: (1) inexhaustible resources such as sunlight and water; (2) renewable resources like plants and animals; (3) nonrenewable resources—most minerals fall into this category; and (4) recyclable resources, including plastic and some minerals.

The word *because* normally does not get a comma before it; it is not a coordinating conjunction (*but, and, for, or, nor, yet,* and *so*) but a lowly subordinating conjunction. This is a common mistake.

For a tutorial on commas and coordinating conjunctions, visit WritingWithSharonWatson.com/commas-compound-sentences-coordinating-conjunctions/ .

The first sentence in his paper is a compound sentence and deserves a comma before the word *and*.

This paper is a solid *C* grade in content and a *C* in grammar/mechanics.

How to Earn a D

It is interesting to see that students who write well with one type of writing might do poorly with another. The following paper is a perfect example of this enigma. The boy in the seventh grade who wrote the following essay did so well with another type of writing that he is featured in the student textbook as an example of how to do something well.

Please read the following persuasive assignment. Then read what this fellow did right and what he did wrong. The word minimum was 300; he wrote 359. The paper appears as he wrote it, except that his copy was double-spaced, as instructed.

What Are Things Coming To?

What are things coming to nowadays I mean, you can't hardly even get a new system with FIFTEEN morally good games. By systems and games I mean video games, the makers are going money crazy. Can't they make enough money by making more E (Everyone) rated games because if they have to make games as bad as some of the ones they do just to survive (which I'm sure they don't) then I would say, "Go work at McDonalds!"

If I were to take 50 randomly selected X-Box games probably only 10-15 (and that's if you're lucky) would be E-rated, *every other one* would be either T (Teen) rated or M (Mature), that's just pitiful! Also, I agree with parents who think that some videogames can make kids more violent.

Imagine this: you get home from school, do your homework, and maybe even fix yourself a little snack, but then you go up to your room and play videogames for a few hours, where all you try to do is kill as many people as you can and get excited when you get a better weapon so you can kill more people. Do you think that some of that might rub off on you? Think long and hard on that one, duh, of course it will, at least a little. And that might, just might have something to do with all the school shootings from teens that are going on. Plus you can never possibly keep up with all the systems & games that keep coming out.

My point on that is because you buy a PlayStation, out comes a PS2, a Nintendo 64, out comes a Gamecube, a PS2, out comes a PS3, I mean it's honestly pathetic. My cousin for example (not to make him look bad, he doesn't have any bad games or anything), keeps getting new stuff. Like he had a PS and a lot of games, then he wanted a PS2. So he traded in his PS and *10 games*, originally worth at least $250 to $300, so he only had to pay 20 dollars for a PS2, which should've only cost $200! And that's supposed to be a good deal! On the other hand though, there are a lot of people kinda like my cousin who don't have any bad games, but there are so many bad games, and they look so cool that some people who don't want to may end up buying 1 or 2 of them. And as a Christian I believe that we shouldn't let ourselves fall for the temptation of the bad games I hope that you will help make this world come to better things, by not playing or buying any evil games, even if your friends do.

CONTENT:

This young writer does a few things right. He defines the ratings on the games just after he mentions them. He also links video game violence to real world violence, something that researchers have successfully done. Transition sentences appear at the end of paragraphs two and three. He includes a call to action in the last sentence. It is clear that he feels strongly about his subject.

However, his writing is like an out-of-control trapeze artist—swinging from one idea to the next—and he is working without a net, which is an outline or at least a list of points in a logical order. It is obvious that he did not list any points before he began writing or arrange any points for a good flow of ideas. Although the reader knows in the first paragraph how the writer feels about the topic, there is no thesis statement on which the reader can focus his attention. This shows that the writer did not write a purpose statement to guide his writing ("I will convince the reader that…").

Such phrases as "the makers are going money crazy," "that's just pitiful!" "duh," "it's honestly pathetic," and so forth, show that the writer is simply yelling at his audience. Ranting and raving is definitely on the Don't List of persuasive writing and should be avoided. Yelling at the reader instead of instructing or leading him automatically lowers the grade.

His one valid point about violence is weakened by the fact that he did not do any research or cite any authorities on the subject. This would have strengthened his argument and made it sound more valid.

Telling a story usually gives a point some muscle, but his scenario and his story only waters down what he had hoped to say.

His concluding paragraph is not separate but added to the fourth paragraph.

What is his paper about? Greedy game makers? The abundance of T- and M-rated games? The violence spawned by playing these games? The proliferation of new game systems and their cost? That Christians shouldn't succumb to the temptation to play violent games? It's hard to tell.

To earn a higher grade, this normally good writer should have narrowed his focus, written a purpose statement for his own benefit, listed his points and ordered them before writing, included a thesis statement in the first paragraph, used his paragraphs to support his points, included research and/or quotations from experts, and finished with a strong call to action—all without yelling at his reader. Writing with a positive, we-can-fix-this attitude is always more effective than using a negative, in-your-face tone.

Summing up, he needs organization, focus, a thesis statement, good format (introductory paragraph, one paragraph for each point in the body, and a concluding paragraph), something in the first paragraph to engage the reader in the topic, facts from research, a clear call to action, and a positive tone.

GRAMMAR/MECHANICS:

This student correctly defines game ratings and capitalizes the names of the game systems.

He uses a double negative in the second sentence. There are many run-on sentences. Students can spot their own run-on sentences easier if they read their paper out loud. This way, they hear where the periods should go.

By using parentheses to add asides, he breaks the flow of his writing. He should use parentheses sparingly and only when needed, as when he defines the video game ratings. Instead of an ampersand (&), he should use the word *and* in paragraph three. A review of comma rules would be helpful.

This is a solid D paper in content and C in grammar/mechanics.

How to Earn an F

Few are the things a student can do to earn an F on a paper. Below is a list of things that, to this teacher's mind, deserve an F. Perhaps you can think of some to add to the list.

- Not doing the assignment
- Not following the directions for the assignment (other than a simple misunderstanding)
- Handing in the assignment very late (Consider subtracting one grade for each day the assignment is late. If the paper is one day late and deserves an A-, give a B+ or a B instead.)
- Plagiarizing

10-Minute Writing Plunges Program

– Guidelines –

- There are enough Writing Plunges (prompts) to last all year.
- 10-Minute Writing Plunges can be a fun break from the workbook or can be used as a year-long program by itself.
- These are designed to encourage reluctant writers and delight eager ones.
- Give a new prompt to your students every Monday, Tuesday, Wednesday, and Thursday. They will write for 10 minutes, keep their own work, and not be graded on it—yet.
- On Friday, students will choose which paper they like best. Then they will proofread it and get it ready to hand in on the following Monday for a grade. However, you can skip this step entirely if you wish. Some students simply need practice writing without being evaluated.
- Avoid using the Writing Plunges while your student is working in the textbook if you think that may be too much writing.
- Students in classroom settings or co-ops may want to read their work aloud.
- Substitute a Grab Bag for a prompt once a month. Put something fun in the bag and have your students write about it (a cookie, an evocative picture, an unusual object, something smelly, and so forth).
- Feel free to substitute your own writing prompts or use the prompts in a different order.
- Enjoy!

10-Minute Writing Plunges for September

Week One

1. Some people celebrate the end of school with something special like a party or a vacation. But what if you celebrated the *beginning* of the school year? Make a plan for a way to celebrate the first day of school. Include a list of supplies, ingredients, tools, activities, or anything else you might need to make this celebration a success.

2. The mayor called the hospital to congratulate Justin in recognition of his courage and heroic actions. But when Justin's mom arrived at the hospital, Justin promised her that he would never again jump into the back of a moving pick-up truck. Write the story about how Justin ended up in the hospital.

3. "I'll never go there again!" (what happened and why you won't go back)

4. You are given a day in which you do not have to do any chores or go anywhere. The whole day is open to you. What will you do?

Week Two

1. "I think the leader of my country should . . ."

2. What book can't you stand? Explain why you won't ever read it again.

3. You have been given $100. There's one catch—you have to give it away. To whom or to what organization will you give it? Then, in a few sentences, explain why you chose that person or organization.

4. The former United States president Franklin D. Roosevelt once said this: "When you reach the end of your rope, tie a knot in it and hang on." Write about a time when you were at the end of your rope. Share the story of what you did at that point. If you are right-handed, write your story with your left hand. If you are left-handed, write your story with your right hand. Your hand writing does not have to be neat. In fact, that may be impossible!

Week Three

1. "If I could cure any disease . . .

2. "God has given me . . .

3. What is the nicest thing someone has done for you or said to you?

4. Monopoly. Farkle. Uno. Rummy. Twister. Chinese checkers. Hide and seek. You've played plenty of games with rules already made up. Now it's your turn

to make up new rules. Choose a familiar game and write new rules for it. Then for a bit of fun, try playing your old game with the new rules.

Week Four

1. "Something good about me is . . .

2. Write an advice column to answer this question from a reader: "I'm lonely, but I want friends. What should I do?"

3. Some people believe it is wrong to eat animals. Others think we should eat anything that is edible. What are your thoughts on the matter? Defend your view of what to eat. Use at least two solid reasons to support your view.

4. "My perfect day is sitting in a room with some blank paper. That's heaven. That's gold." That quote is from author Cormac McCarthy. What is your idea of a perfect day? Choose the form in which you want to write about it: poem, essay, short story, journal entry, and so forth.

10-Minute Writing Plunges for October

Week One

1. "A smart thing I once did was . . .

2. Trounced. Obliterated. Sunk. Blasted. Squeaked out. Outlasted. All of these words are the colorful verbs sportscasters use to describe how a team won a game. For instance, "The Tigers squeaked out a 5-to-4 win against the Cougars" or "The Hotdogs annihilated the Berries in a 17-to-2 landslide." Make a list of five other verbs you can use in place of "won" or "lost."

3. Think about the main character in a favorite book or movie. What has the writer done to get you on the main character's side or to make that character likeable? Make a list.

4. What would you put on a bumper sticker? Use ten words or fewer.

Week Two

1. Words of opposite meaning are called antonyms. For instance, *difficult* is one antonym for *easy*. Look up the word *lucid* and then write three antonyms for it. Use one of the antonyms in a sentence.

2. Fall is known for specific scents: pumpkins, spices, cider, and so on. But what about smells you do not like? Write about a smell or odor you can't stand.

3. Write a humorous story about a stupid or embarrassing thing you once did.

4. You won an RV or camper trailer for a week. Write a journal entry of one of your days with it.

Week Three

1. Peter encourages us in I Peter 5:7 to cast all of our cares on the Lord because He cares for us. If you had a box to put your cares in and give to the Lord, what would you put in the box?

2. "A habit I'd like to break is . . ."

3. What advice would you like to give someone?

4. Imagine you are a parent. Write a note to convince your child to do a particular chore.

Week Four

1. Draw the floor plan of your house. Put another family in it and describe one of their meals together. Write their conversation.

2. You are in a job interview. Describe yourself to the interviewer. Ignore physical descriptions and go for other attributes or features of yourself that will make you a winning employee.

3. What superpower do you wish you had? How would you use it?

4. Write a radio ad to convince listeners to adopt a shelter pet.

10-Minute Writing Plunges for November

Week One

1. Imagine that teachers and students all over the world are switching places with each other today. Write out the dialog of one student trying to teach a teacher something.

2. Write about a special talent or trait you have.

3. You are writing a children's book entitled *Come Back*. Write the first paragraph.

4. What is the opposite of love? Explain.

Week Two

1. Write a prayer of thanks to God.

2. You are outside today, and something falls from the sky with a note attached to it. You grab the item, open the note, and read this: "You'll get one of these a day for a month." What is the "something" that falls from the sky? Write the story of what happens or write what you would like to have fall from the sky each day for a month.

3. Invent a children's cereal. Name it and write a TV commercial for it.

4. Describe a real hike you have taken or a pretend walk in the woods.

Week Three

1. You have an opportunity to go overseas. Which country will you choose? What will you do there?

2. Write a greeting card for a holiday. Decorate it, if you wish.

3. You have been given a pair of experimental anti-gravity boots for your birthday, and you had a load of fun breaking them in. However, last Thursday you found yourself in a strange circumstance you had not anticipated. What does your journal entry or diary say on last Thursday's page?

4. An elderly neighbor left you a barn in his or her will. What condition is the barn in? What does it contain? What are you going to do with it?

Week Four

1. You are an imaginary creature—fairy, Thor, leprechaun, troll, giant, talking animal, Bigfoot, and so on. You have a message of great importance to tell a particular human but you can communicate only in poetry. Write a poem to tell this person your urgent message.

2. Ted Williams, a famous Boston Red Sox baseball player, had his body frozen when he died. Did he hope to have his body thawed out and fixed when new advances in medicine would make it possible for him to live again? He is not the only one to have his body cryogenically frozen. Celebrities like Muhammad Ali and Simon Cowell have mentioned that they, too, would like to have their bodies frozen to be revived later. Should people have their bodies frozen so they possibly can be revived later? What's your opinion on this matter?

3. Write a letter to a friend (real or imagined) who is discouraged.

4. You found bad news when you researched your family tree. What did you find? Who will you tell and how?

10-Minute Writing Plunges for December

Week One

1. A grandparent just bought a mobile phone like the one you or your family uses. Explain to him or her how to call someone. Make a list of the steps. Older students: Also make a clear list of the steps of how to attach an image to a text.

2. "My favorite thing to talk about is . . ."

3. Write a story that begins like this: "The sound had stopped, but the air still vibrated with the shock of its disturbance."

4. You just gave someone a gift, but he or she doesn't like it. Write the conversation that ensues between you both.

Week Two

1. In *Warriors Don't Cry*, Melba Pattillo Beals tells about a Christmas tradition her family had. Each one would take a personal item and give it to someone in need. Sometimes this was painful because Melba's mother or grandmother would encourage her to give away a favorite item. You are going to take one item from your bedroom and give it to someone else. What is it, and to whom will you give it?

2. On the left side of your paper, write everyone's name in your family. Next to each name, write one thing about him or her that you like or admire.

3. The Bible has been read in many interesting places, but on Christmas Eve in 1968, it was read from a spacecraft while orbiting the moon.

On December 24, 1968, during the most-watched television broadcast to date, three astronauts read Genesis 1:1-10 to a mesmerized world and then ended their message with this: "And from the crew of Apollo 8, we close with good night, good luck, a Merry Christmas – and God bless all of you, all of you on the good Earth."

If you were in outer space and read a portion of the Bible to the Earthlings, which passage would you choose? Jot down your ideas.

4. If you were to meet someone from the original Christmas story, who would you like to meet? What would you do together? What would you ask him or her? What would you tell him or her? You can find the accounts of Jesus' birth in Matthew 1-2, Luke 1:26-38, and Luke 2:1-40.

10-Minute Writing Plunges for January

Week One

1. Harry Houdini, the famous escape artist, said this about his plans for himself: "Vigorous self-training, to enable me to do remarkable things with my body, to make not one muscle or a group of muscles but every muscle a responsive worker, quick and sure . . .." Harry instructed his brother to tie him up so he could practice escaping, and he taught himself how to tie and untie knots with his toes. What skill would you like to learn in this new year? It can be anywhere from silly to serious.

2. What do you like to do to make someone happy?

3. Close your eyes or put a bandanna over them for 5 minutes. Pretend you are blind. What do you hear? Write your impressions.

4. What is the worst thing someone can say to someone else?

Week Two

1. The man we know today as Martin Luther King Jr. was not born with that name. His original name was Michael King Jr., and he was known as Little Mike when he was young. It is not known for sure how Little Mike became Martin Luther King, but the story goes that after his father visited the Holy Land and Europe, he legally changed his name and his son's name to Martin Luther King to reflect what he had just learned about the reformer Martin Luther. If you were to change your name to reflect something important you've learned or something of importance to you, what would your new name be? Write your idea and explain it in a paragraph or two.

2. Write a prayer for someone.

3. You are going on a trip, but you can only take five things with you. What will you take and why? (No fair listing a full backpack or a bulging piece of luggage as one of your five items!)

4. The most important of the Ten Commandments to me is _____ because...

Week Three

1. Make a list of five adjectives that describe your last trip to the dentist.

2. You are starting a business. Money is supplied to you, so that is no problem. What business would you like to start? What will be your specialty? Jot down some ideas. Then design a logo, a short motto, and a name for your business.

3. Ask two adults in your life how they had fun as kids. Then record their answers. Did you learn something interesting? Shocking? After you have recorded their answers, write your reactions to what you learned.

4. Write a list of five things you believe about God.

Week Four

1. That first, fateful night when Dr. Victor Frankenstein created his monster, his creation ran away. The two did not meet again for a few years. Write the dialog of the doctor and the monster at their first meeting in years.

2. Design a new coin. Write a letter to the government and tell them why they should use your coin and design.

3. Skip a meal (if you are medically able to) and write what it feels like.

4. Look around you: this room, this day, these people, those possessions or items, that music. In 15 years, what do you think you will remember about today?

10-Minute Writing Plunges for February

Week One

1. "I was very embarrassed when . . ."

2. Describe the sequence of events in a thunderstorm. The day starts out sunny. Take it from there. Use as many senses as possible. Rainbows are optional!

3. "My pet peeves are . . ."

4. Write out a favorite Bible verse and explain why you like it.

Week Two

1. Laura Ingalls Wilder, author of the Little House series, wrote that she became her sister Mary's eyes when Mary lost her sight. Pretend you are looking at a person, a location, or an item for someone else. Describe it for them. Use color, size, shape, texture, and other clues to help them visualize it.

2. Write the last paragraph of a story about castaways.

3. Two characters are trapped in a cave. One has a plan to escape. The other disagrees with that plan and wants to get out another way. Write their story of how they try to escape the cave while hotly disagreeing.

4. "Television is the national campfire around which we spend our time." (Bill Moyers) Make a list of ways that sitting around the television is similar to sitting around a campfire. Then make a list of ways it is different.

Week Three

1. "I can't wait to be older so I can . . ."

2. If it were possible to know what would happen tomorrow, would you want to know? Explain. "

3. If you could travel with a group like a circus, a music group, a sports team, a chess club, a politician's entourage, and so forth, what group would you travel with? Choose a group and then describe what it would be like to travel with it for one day.

4. If a character feels sad, a good writer will avoid telling readers this: "Ricardo felt sad." In other words, they won't *tell* the reader how the character feels; they'll *show* the reader what the character does, like this: "When Ricardo struck out and made the last out of the game, his shoulders slumped and he dropped his bat." Think about what people do when they feel very happy. Then write a sentence showing what a character could do when he or she feels happy.

Week Four

1. The easiest thing in the world for me to do is . . ."

2. In Greek mythology, Daedalus attached wings to himself and his son Icarus to escape exile. He used feathers and affixed them with wax. Daedalus warned Icarus not to fly too close to the sun, but, of course, the boy did. When the wax melted from the heat of the sun, Icarus's feathers came loose, and he plummeted into the sea and died. The Icarian Sea is named for him. Write about a time you were warned about something. How did it turn out? (Better than Icarus, I hope!)

3. Write the journal entry of a teacher on a particularly difficult day.

4. Describe a friend or family member in terms of a weather forecast.

10-Minute Writing Plunges for March

Week One

1. Write your opinion of a sports figure of your choice.

2. Write about one thing you did today and why you want someone to know about it.

3. There is too much _____ in the world today. Explain.

4. What item from your childhood do you treasure? Write a short story using it as the main character.

Week Two

1. Invent a warning that will go on a sign or a product. Draw a picture, if necessary.

2. If you were to do a favor for a grouch today, what would it be?

3. "When I am 25, I am going to . . ."

4. Change the ending of a familiar movie. Make the characters do something else.

Week Three

1. Saint Patrick, whom we celebrate in March, is famous for teaching the ancient Irish about Christianity in the fifth century. Legend has it that in order to teach people about the Holy Trinity (Father, Son, and Holy Spirit), Patrick used a three-leaf shamrock to show how each leaf is separate but also part of the same plant. It is a wise person who can use simple items to teach important truths about God. Jesus did this often when he used pearls, coins, sheep, and other everyday objects to teach others about their Father. Choose something from your house or your life and use it to teach a truth from the Bible. Write down your object and also the lesson you want it to represent.

2. Choose a game you are familiar with. Write the instructions for how to play it.

3. Write a section of the story of Snow White from a dwarf's point of view.

4. What bugs you? Write a poem about it.

Week Four

1. List all the foods, snacks, fruits, drinks, spices, and flavorings that begin with the letter "P."

2. You are a famous meteorologist. Invent and write tomorrow's weather forecast.

3. If you could have three wishes, what would they be?

4. You work in a theme park or an amusement park. What is your job? Explain. Possibilities: graphic designer for the tickets and online ads, wear an animal costume all day, work in a concession stand, security, work the rides, design the rides, medic, and so forth.

10-Minute Writing Plunges for April

Week One

1. "The next time I get the chance, I'm going to . . ."

2. List the traits or habits of a good driver.

3. Design a new traffic sign. Draw the shape of the sign and what goes on it. Write a TV commercial to explain to the public what it means.

4. Write a Sunday school lesson on Psalm 23.

Week Two

1. You won a contest, and your family gets to go on an all-expense-paid trip. Where will you go? Write about your exciting plans.

2. What makes your heart pound?

3. Write a conversation between two people who have just had a car accident with one other.

4. "I'm too old to . . . "

Week Three

1. Read Jesus' parable of the prodigal son in Luke 15:11-32. Which character do you identify with in the story? Explain.

2. "The things I love to hear are . . . "

3. You are old enough to have lived through something difficult: losing a pet, breaking a bone, moving to a new location, being in a car accident, experiencing something catastrophic like an earthquake, and so forth. Write your story of how you lived through the difficult situation.

4. Write a story using all the words from your spelling list.

Week Four

1. "I would regret it if I never . . ."

2. The Psalms in the Bible are poems and were sung in their original language of Hebrew. They do not rhyme, and they didn't rhyme in the original Hebrew. Those poets relied on rhythms and devices such as repetition for their poetry. Get your Bible and read Psalm 100. Then write it as a poem that rhymes.

3. Which sport would you compete in if you were in the winter or summer Olympics?

4. You are usually on the receiving end of grades. Now you get to make some up. Make a report card for yourself. Invent subjects. Give yourself grades in these new subjects.

10-Minute Writing Plunges for May

Week One

1. If you could have an artist paint a picture for you, what would you have the artist paint? Explain.

2. "What time I am afraid, I will trust in thee" (Psalm 56:3 KJV). Write about a time when you were afraid. What were you afraid of? What happened? What helped you get through that scary time?

3. Peter Pan left his mother at an early age. In fact, he was only a baby, according to his creator, Sir James Barrie. Because of this early separation, Peter Pan had a hard time understanding what a mother is and what she does. Write a list of things a mother is and what she does so you can explain the concept of mothers to Peter Pan. Your list does not need to be in complete sentences.

4. Something you just bought isn't right. Write a letter to the store or manufacturer.

Week Two

1. You just won a shopping spree at a store. Which store? What will you buy?

2. In Ray Bradbury's science-fiction short story "I Sing the Body Electric," a family loses a mother and desires to fill their needs with a grandmother, so they have one built for them. They are able to order the qualities they want her to have. If you were to order a grandmother robot, what would you program her to look like? What would she do? What qualities would she have? What would her

personality be like? What would she enjoy doing? Write down your ideas or write a short story of your own about ordering a robot "person."

3. Write a sermon based on anything you find in Psalm 139.

4. You are visiting the zoo when you hear an announcement cautioning everyone that an animal has escaped. What animal has escaped? What do you do next? Write your story.

Week Three

1. You hear your pet talking. What is he/she saying?

2. Pretend you have a scar. Or think about one you have. How did you get it?

3. "I often pray about/for . . ."

4. List five words at random from any book. Then write a story that includes all five.

Week Four

1. Write a blurb (the stuff on the back cover) for your favorite book. Don't give away the ending!

2. You're going to a sporting event. Would you rather be a player on the team, a coach, a referee or umpire, a parent cheering a player on, an owner or manager, an announcer making the play-by-play calls, a photographer of the game, a concession-stand worker, a fan, or other participant? Make your choice and then explain why you chose it.

3. If you were to witness a miracle, what would you like to see?

4. People disagree on many things: politics, religion, global climate change, favorite vehicle brand, or whether to use mayonnaise or mustard on their sandwiches. We all have our own opinions and preferences. Name one thing that everyone can agree on. Then write two to three sentences to defend your selection.

Answer Key

Answers to Daily Lessons
Essay Assignments
Suggested Writing Schedules

Get Your Feet Wet

Skill 1: What do you think?

Students are answering personal questions about writing. Answers will vary.

Skill 2: Brainstorm

Students are using sticky notes or the cluster method to brainstorm the benefits of owning a pet. Answers will vary.

Skill 3: Write then fix

Students are writing for 10 minutes on either the best day they've ever had or a pet peeve/annoying habit. Answers will vary.

Opinions—You've Got Them

Skill 1: What do you think?

Students are filling in at least 5 sets of favorites or least favorites in a chart. Answers will vary

Skill 2: Reasons

Students are writing a personal opinion and three reasons why they hold it.

What are the three reasons that came up in the soccer conversation?
1. He has shown talent by breaking a league record.

2. He feels he was born to play soccer.

3. His parents and coach are all supporting him.

Skill 3: Point order

Students are writing an opinion, five reasons they hold it, selecting an effective point order, and rearranging three of their five reasons. Answers will vary

Skill 4: The body

Students are reading a sample opinion essay about cats and listing two supporting statements the writer uses to prove cats are clean:

They constantly lick themselves clean.
They can be trained to use a kitty litter box.

Students are also selecting one of their reasons from Skill 3, writing it up in a complete sentence as a topic sentence, and writing the rest of the paragraph.

Skill 5: Paragraphs and topic sentences

Students are given three choices of exercises and told to use the Create Your Own Paragraph to develop and write a paragraph. Your copy of Create Your Own Paragraph is on page 13 of the Teacher's Guide.

Skill 6: Paragraph types and examples

Write a paragraph in the form of an interrogatory, climactic, process, or enumerative paragraph and then label it.

Skill 7: Introductory paragraph

Write an introductory paragraph for the opinion you chose in Skill 1, the topic you used with your paragraph chart in Skill 5, or choose another topic. Use one of the tools you just learned: an interesting statement, fact, quotation, question, or story. Make sure the readers know whether you are for or against the topic.

Skill 8: Concluding paragraph

Write a satisfying conclusion to the introduction you wrote in Skill 7. Use any of the five tools. Try to tie your introduction to your conclusion.

Skill 9: Evaluate this student's opinion

1. Does she have an interesting first sentence? *Personal opinion; one hopes "yes."*

2. How does she tie her conclusion to her introduction? *She calls the cello her peg-legged friend again.*

3. In paragraphs four and five, what are her reasons for liking the cello? *Paragraph 4: the teacher. Paragraph 5: She likes to perform.*

4. How many paragraphs are in her introduction? *Two. Sometimes one paragraph is not enough.*

5. Fill in the blank: She makes playing the cello seem _____. *Possible words: interesting, hard work, exciting, personally rewarding, and so on.*

Skill 10: The assignment

CHOOSE ONE:

❑ Complete and polish the opinion you have been working on. Word count: at least 150 words. Experienced writers: at least 200 words.

❑ Do you love to write? Can't stand it? Write your opinion of writing. Use at least 150 words. Experienced writers: at least 200 words.

❑ The writer of "My New Pet" really likes cats. Do you disagree with the writer? Write your opinion of your favorite animal or pet. Or write why you detest cats. Use at least 150 words. Experienced writers: at least 200 words.

❏ Look at the favorite/least-favorite lists you filled out in Skill 1. Choose one of those topics and write your opinion about it in at least 150 words. Experienced writers: at least 200 words.

❏ Your choice. Choose something that you love or can't stand (something you feel strongly about) and write why you hold that opinion. Use at least 150 words. Experienced writers: at least 200 words.

A suggested writing schedule

Check off each day's task as you complete it:

Day 1: Brainstorm opinions you hold. Choose one of them and brainstorm possible reasons for it. Decide on your three strongest ones and an order in which to put them.

Days 2-3: Write the body (the three paragraphs that include your three reasons).

Day 4: Write the introduction and conclusion.

Day 5: Combine the intro, body, and conclusion. Proofread and revise with the checklist on the next page. Make a neat copy, double-spaced, either by hand or on a computer. Hand it in.

News Flash: For every one hundred words you are assigned, it's going to take at least one hour of thinking and writing. So for a one-hundred-fifty-word essay, you'll need at least one-and-a-half hours. Leave yourself plenty of time to do each daily task.

Skill 11: Use this checklist

Students have a checklist aimed at training them to proofread their own work and to see if the essay stacks up to the instructions. The most important thing they can to do catch mistakes and make revisions is to **print off their paper and read it aloud**.

TEACHER: CHECK AT THE END OF EACH DAY TO SEE IF YOUR STUDENT HAS COMPLETED THAT DAY'S TASK. THAT WAY, THE ESSAY ISN'T ONE HUGE ASSIGNMENT; IT IS A SERIES OF SMALL, ACHIEVABLE STEPS.

Teacher: Your grading grid for this opinion essay assignment is on page 92 and is similar to the student's checklist.

Persuasion: The basics

Skill 1: Words can be powerful

Students are writing about a time they tried to persuade someone: what the topic was, what their reasons were, and if it worked.

Skill 2: Choose a topic

Students are brainstorming topics they feel strongly about and then writing a purpose statement concerning one of them.

Skill 3: Choose reasons

Students are listing a great/horrible book or movie and five reasons why the library should buy it or not buy it.

Skill 4: Put them in an order

Students are arranging their top three book/movie points into two point orders and deciding which one works better for their set of reasons and their audience.

Skill 5: Prove or explain

Students are choosing one of their points, creating a topic sentence from it, and writing a paragraph using their tools of facts, stories, quotations, examples, and statements. They are encouraged to use the form Create Your Own Paragraph in My Locker in their textbook. Your copy of the empty form is on page 13.

Skill 6: Refuting an argument

Students are refuting an argument on the topic of being a vegetarian or an omnivore.

Skill 7: Persuasive introduction

Students are writing an introduction for the topic they wrote about in Skill 5.

Skill 8: Persuasive conclusion

Students are writing a conclusion for the topic they wrote about in Skill 5. They also are tying the conclusion to the intro and issuing a call to action.

Skill 9: Evaluate this student's essay

1. Does his first sentence make you want to read more? *Personal opinion.*

2. List the five reasons why he likes Spider-Man. *1) lots of action, 2) exciting movie, 3) suspense, 4) explains where he got his powers, 5) strong villain*

3. If you have seen the movie, do you agree with his reasons? *Personal opinion*

4. If you have not seen the movie, do his reasons make you want to see it? *Personal opinion*

5. Have you heard anything that is negative about this movie? If so, what are the negative things that this boy didn't include? *Answers will vary.*

6. Write the purpose statement this writer might have used as he wrote his essay. *I am going to convince the reader that Spider-Man is a good movie to watch.*

7. What was his call to action? *Watch the movie or watch it again.*

8. Based on what you now know about persuasive writing, what grade would you give him? *Personal opinion; one hopes an A.*

Teacher, in giving a grade to a fellow student, it is important for your student to evaluate the essay based on its strength, not on whether your student agrees with the opinion expressed in it.

Skill 10: Persuasion guidelines

Students are reading a Don't List and a Do List for persuasive writing and identifying any guidelines they are interested in or ones that surprised them.

Skill 11: Proofreading

Important information about proofreading as it appears in the student textbook:

There is no need to look for all mistakes and changes at once. Let me say that again: Do not try to fix everything the first time you read through your essay. Follow this schedule:

- First, write your essay a day or two before it is due. That way, you can look at it later with fresh eyes to catch mistakes and make changes.
- Second, break up the tasks. Read through your essay first for any changes you want to make in what you said and how you expressed it. This is called the **content**.
- Then read through your essay again and look for one potential trouble spot at a time: punctuation, spelling, commas, run-on sentences, and so on. This is called **mechanics**.
- Last, read through it a third time, out loud, to catch anything else that needs to be changed. Make your revisions.

Students are getting their first look at the proofreading tool Mistake Medic. They are also proofreading a previous essay of their choice. If they already used the checklist in "Opinions—You've Got Them," which dealt with content, then they are to proceed to the checklist below. This is taken directly from Mistake Medic. Students have Mistake Medic on page 57 and in their section labeled My Locker. You have a copy of it on page 9.

2. Check your title for correct capital letters. Don't underline it or put quotation marks around it. Skip a line after the title.

3. Is your paper double-spaced?

4. Did you indent (five spaces) the first line of every paragraph?

5. Read your paper aloud. Is anything confusing? Add words or change them as necessary.

6. Look for unnecessarily repeated words. Use specific adjectives and nouns and powerful verbs. But don't get fancy.

7. Look for run-on sentences and sentence fragments.

8. Make sure all of your commas are there for a reason, not just because you want to pause or have to hiccup. Check your other punctuation. Refer to your grammar book.

9. Check your capital letters. Every sentence begins with one. Proper nouns need one.

10. Circle possible spelling and homonym mistakes (*there, their,* and *they're,* for example). Then look them up in a dictionary.

Make the necessary revisions and hand in both copies—the original and the revised one.

Students are given a page of Hot Proofreading Tips:

Avoid writing your paper the night before it is due. If you **write it a day or two earlier**, your paper has time to "cool off." You can read through your paper with an objective eye, catching mistakes and revising the way you expressed your thoughts.

Read your paper out loud. Read every word. You may be surprised at how many mistakes you can catch this way.

Resize the font. This moves everything around so you can see any mistakes quickly.

Ask a friend to read your paper. He or she may find something that doesn't make sense.

Print your paper instead of reading it from the screen. When you read the hard copy, you find many more mistakes.

Proofread your paper in **a different location** from where you wrote it. This gives you a clearer mind when checking for possible revisions.

Have you been told that you have a problem with run-on sentences? One of the best ways to find where the period goes is to **read your paper out loud.** Somehow, your ear catches it and you know where to end the sentence.

Label your sentence structures to make sure you haven't used the same ones over and over again.

Count the number of words in each sentence. Put the numbers in the margin. If all the numbers are similar, consider varying some of your sentence lengths. If some numbers are significantly over 20, check for run-on sentences or rewrite them to make your point clearer and concise.

Teacher, the following are links to **grammar and proofreading tutorials** on Writing with Sharon Watson:

https://writingwithsharonwatson.com/grammar-tutorials-bundle/

https://writingwithsharonwatson.com/proofreading-tutorials-bundle/

https://writingwithsharonwatson.com/estore/grammar-lets-eat-ebook/

Skill 12: The assignment

CHOOSE ONE:

☐ Finish the original topic you chose in Skill 2. **Persuade** your readers to change their minds or do something specific. Word count: at least 200 words. Experienced writers: 250 words.

❏ Finish the letter to the librarian about the great/horrible movie or book. **Persuade** him or her to buy the book for the library (or not buy it). When you finish this assignment, consider calling your local library for the name of the library's purchaser. Then mail your letter to him or her. Word count: at least 200 words. Experienced writers: 250 words.

❏ Your choice. Choose a topic you care about and use your new skills to **persuade** the reader to believe and behave a certain way. Word count: at least 200 words. Experienced writers: at least 250 words.

A suggested writing schedule

Check off each section as you complete it:

Day 1: Brainstorm ideas. Decide on your topic, three reasons, an order, and a purpose statement.

Days 2-3: Create three topic sentences from your three reasons. Then write the supporting statements for the three separate paragraphs in the body.

Day 4: Write the introduction and conclusion. Your conclusion will include a call to action (something specific your reader can do).

Day 5: Arrange the paragraphs in order of introduction, body, and conclusion. Proofread three separate times using the checklist on the next page and Mistake Medic in My Locker. Revise as needed. Make a neat, double-spaced copy and hand it in.

Skill 13: Use this checklist

Students are using a specific checklist that will aid them in the proofreading and revising process.

Teacher: Your grading grid for this persuasive-essay assignment is on page 93 and is similar to the student's checklist.

Cause and Effect

Note: This cause-and-effect essay is a persuasive one. Students must choose a side and defend it.

Skill 1: What cause and effect means

Students are choosing an invention, deciding if it has been beneficial or harmful to us, and writing five points to prove their decision.

Skill 2: Choose an effective order

Students are writing a purpose statement for their beneficial or harmful invention.

And now they are choosing an effective order in which to arrange their points: inverted pyramid, climactic, chronological, or effect size.

Skill 3: A strong body

Students are choosing one of their points, developing a topic sentence and then supporting statements to complete one paragraph about their chosen invention.

Skill 4: Introduction and conclusion

Students are writing an introduction and a conclusion for their topic of the helpful or harmful invention.

Skill 5: Evaluate this student's essay

1. Does the first sentence interest you? *Personal opinion*

2. How does the writer let you know the refrigerator is a beneficial invention without saying, "The refrigerator is good"? *By writing about it in a positive light: "ice-cold sodas," "fresh garden vegetables," "handy refrigerators," and "wonderful ways it would be used."*

3. Is the last sentence a good one to end with? *Personal opinion. It was clever, and it tied in with the first sentence.*

4. What are the writer's three reasons why the refrigerator is beneficial? *1) helps the medical profession, 2) healthier lifestyles, 3) makes flowers and floral arrangements more available*

5. What order does the writer use for the reasons? *Inverted pyramid*

6. For paragraphs 2-4, name the types of paragraphs they are, based on your knowledge of paragraph types: direct, interrogatory, climactic, process, and enumerative. *Paragraph 2 is interrogatory. Paragraph 3 is direct. Paragraph 4 is climactic.*

7. Based on your knowledge of cause and effect, what grade would you give this student? *Answers will vary; possibly an A.*

Skill 6: The assignment

CHOOSE ONE:

☐ Finish the cause-and-effect persuasive paper you have already begun. Put the paragraphs in an order that will persuade your readers. Word count: at least 250 words. Experienced writers: at least 300 words.

☐ Choose some other invention. Determine whether you want to show its harmful effects on the world **or** positive effects. Write your persuasive paper to prove your point. Word count: at least 250 words. Experienced writers: at least 300 words.

☐ Your choice. Choose another cause-and-effect topic and write a persuasive paper on the positive things **or** negative things that have happened because of it. Word count: at least 250 words. Experienced writers: at least 300 words.

A suggested writing schedule

Check off each task as you complete it:

Day 1: **Brainstorm.** Decide on your invention/topic. Decide whether it has been beneficial or harmful to the world. Brainstorm points and save three strong ones.

Day 2: **Research** your invention/topic and keep a brief history of it for your introduction.

Days 3-4: **Write** the supporting statements for your reasons in three separate paragraphs. Refer to your research notes, if necessary. Use the Create Your Own Paragraph chart in My Locker, if you wish. Choose an effective point order.

Day 5: **Write** the introduction and conclusion. Include the brief history, the inventor, and something to indicate that this invention has been helpful or harmful. Include a call to action in the conclusion.

Day 6: **Proofread** three separate times and revise using the checklist on the next page. Make a neat, double-spaced copy.

Skill 7: Use this checklist

Students are directed to write down their purpose statement in the textbook. In addition, they are to print off their essay and read it aloud to catch more mistakes and make revisions. This is part of their training in proofreading.

Teacher: The grading grid for this cause-and-effect persuasive essay is on page 94 and is similar to the student's checklist.

A Newspaper Article

Skill 1: Fact versus opinion

Students are reading statements and labeling them either "F" for fact or "O" for opinion.

1. F	4. O	7. O	10. O	13. O
2. O	5. O	8. F	11. F	14. F
3. F	6. O	9. O	12. F	

Skill 2: Inverted pyramid

Students are writing the lead for an interesting event, including Who, What, Where, When, Why, and How.

Skill 3: An outer-space example

Students are labeling Who, What, Where, When, Why, and How:

    Where   **What**
MOJAVE, Calif. (AP) –An ungainly-looking rocket plane punched through the Earth's
                    When   **Why (or What)**
atmosphere and then glided home to a desert landing Monday in history's first privately financed

manned spaceflight – a voyage that could hasten the day when the final frontier is opened up to

paying customers.
    Who   **How**   **Where again**
Pilot Mike Melvill took SpaceShipOne 62.2 miles above Earth, just a little more than 400 feet

above the distance considered to be the boundary of space.

Skill 4: The significance

Students are writing the lead for a Bible account of their choice, including the 5Ws, the H, and the significance.

Skill 5: The rest of the story

Students are reading Genesis 1:26-31 and Genesis 2:7-25 to answer the following questions:

1. **Who** did it? *God*

2. **What** did he do? *Created a man and then a woman*

3. **When** did he do it? *On the sixth day*

4. **Where** did he do it? *The man—outside Eden; the woman—inside the Garden of Eden*

5. **Why** did he do it? *More research is needed.*

6. **How** did he do it? *The man—from the dust of the ground; the woman—from the man's rib.*

Skill 6: Attributions

Students are writing attributions for four sources. Answers will vary. Here are some possibilities:

1. "I was young and ignorant, and I envied my brother," admitted Mark Twain in his autobiography *Roughing It.*

2. According to www.canalmuseum.com, the official Internet site for the Panama Canal, "A ship traveling from New York to San Francisco can save 7,872 miles using the Panama Canal instead of going around South America."

3. C. S. Lewis, author of *The Lion, the Witch, and the Wardrobe*, revealed that he created the faun Mr. Tumnus from a dream he had in his teens.

4. "The ground was rolling under my feet. I felt like I was on a boat," reported 13-year-old earthquake survivor Maritza Ruiz.

Skill 7: The Assignment

CHOOSE ONE:

☐ Finish the news article for which you wrote the lead in Skill 2. Use facts, not opinions. When you add the lead and the significance to the rest of the article, the total word count should be 200-300 words.

☐ Choose a historical account from the Bible, like the example of David ben Jesse. Write the lead, including the significance of the event. Then write the rest of the story in short paragraphs. You don't have to retell the whole story. Just write the highlights that people will want to know about. Use facts, not opinions. Word count: 200-300 words.

A suggested writing schedule

Check off each section as you complete it:

Day 1: Decide on which story you will write up. Read all you can about it to get plenty of facts. Take notes and record your sources.

Day 2: Write the lead. Include the five Ws, the H, and the significance of the event.

Day 3: Write the rest of the article chronologically. Use short paragraphs, simple sentences, past-tense verbs, and attributions for facts or quotes.

Day 4: Put the lead and the story together. Proofread and revise three times using the checklist on the next page. Make a neat, double-spaced copy.

Skill 8: Use this checklist

Students are using a checklist to make sure they have followed the instructions and revised where needed.

Teacher: Your grading grid for a newspaper article is on page 95. The student checklist is similar to the grading grid.

A How-to

Skill 1: I know how to do this

Students are checking activities they know how to do.

Students are also writing instructions on how to make a peanut butter and jelly sandwich. This can be done individually or as a group.

For fun, get another group of people to perform the steps on the list to see if it is effective.

Skill 2: Evaluate this student

1. Could you make a peanut butter and jelly sandwich from their list? *Personal opinion; however, the list is close to complete.*

2. Revise any steps or add any they left out. *Wash your hands before beginning.*

3. If you wanted to tell your readers some fun things to add to a peanut butter sandwich (other than jelly), where would you add that information? *Most likely after item 5.*

4. Based on the order and completeness of their list, what grade would you give these students? *Personal opinion; most likely an A or B.*

Skill 3: The essay method, part 1

Students are selecting a how-to topic, choosing a specific audience and tone, and writing an introduction.

Skill 4: The essay method, part 2

Fill in the blanks:

1. Write an <u>introduction</u>.

2. List <u>items</u> or <u>ingredients</u>.

3. Go <u>step</u> by <u>step</u>.

4. Be <u>clear</u>.

Students are evaluating the following how-to essay by a student. Circle his list of ingredients. Underline his transition words and phrases. Put numbers next to his steps; are they chronological? Put an arrow next to the sentence in which he tells you how to use your chalk.

How to Make Homemade Chalk

You will need the following items: an empty toilet paper tube, 1 ¼ cups plaster of Paris, waxed paper, a disposable container (such as a 15 oz. or larger margarine tub), a plastic spoon, ½ cup water, and, finally, tempera paint. 1. <u>First</u>, line the inside of your toilet paper tube with waxed paper and set the tube upright on another sheet of waxed paper. 2. <u>Next</u>, make the plaster. Mix together the water and plaster of Paris in the disposable container. 3. <u>When the mixture is smooth,</u> add several spoonsful of paint until you get the color you like. (I used six spoonsful of yellow paint and three spoonsful of red paint to make the color orange.) 4. <u>After you've completed that</u>, use a plastic spoon to put the plaster in the tube. 5.Gently tap the tube to remove any air bubbles.

6. <u>When you are done</u>, throw away the container and the spoon.   Be careful not to get any plaster down your sink because it will dry and clog up your pipes!

<u>After twenty-four hours</u>, the plaster should be dry. 7. Carefully peel away the tube from the chalk and take the chalk out of the waxed paper.

✓ Have fun drawing!

1. Does this writer leave out anything? *An introductory paragraph*

2. What does he do well? *Lists the ingredients, goes step by step, uses transition phrases, and tells you what to do with the chalk.*

3. Based on what you know about a how-to, what grade would you give him? *Personal opinion; possibly an A.*

Skill 5: The instruction-manual method

Students are reading how to bake a cake in the instruction-manual method. They are to underline the student's imperative verbs: 1. <u>Wash</u>, 2. <u>Preheat</u>, 3. <u>Get</u>, 4. <u>Gather</u>, 5. <u>Pour</u>, 6. <u>Measure and pour</u>, 7. <u>Add</u>, 8. <u>Turn</u>, 9. <u>Pour</u>, 10. <u>Bake</u>, 11. <u>Ice</u>, 12. <u>Cut and enjoy</u>.

Skill 6: The assignment

CHOOSE ONE:

❒ Write a how-to in the essay method. Use 300-500 words. Include images or charts, if necessary.

❒ Write a how-to in the Instruction-Manual Method. Use 150-300 words. Include images or charts, if necessary.

A suggested writing schedule

Check off each section as you complete it:

Day 1: Decide what you want to teach. Choose your audience. Write your list of steps.

Days 2-3: Decide on your method. Write your paper.

Day 4: Reread to make sure your steps are in the right order and that you have not forgotten any steps. Create any charts or images you may need.

Day 5: Proofread and revise three separate times for mistakes and needed changes. Use one of the checklists on the next page. Make a neat, double-spaced copy of your paper. Write your intended audience on your paper.

Skill 7: Use one of these checklists

Students choose which checklist to use based on which how-to they are writing.

Teacher: The grading grids for a how-to, both essay and instruction-manual method, are on pages 96 and 97. Students' checklists are similar to your grading grids.

A Report

Skill 1: What is a report?

Students are reading a good-sized paragraph from a nonfiction source, collecting facts from the paragraph, closing the book, and writing the paragraph from their list of facts.

Skill 2: Reconstruct a paragraph

Students are cutting apart a page from the textbook, one sentence at a time, and trying to reconstruct a paragraph in its original order. Here is the original order:

The calendar that we use today hasn't always been around. At first, people kept track of the year by the seasons. They knew that things began to grow again at the same time every year. Today we call that season *spring*. Later, people paid attention to the moon and its phases (new moon, full moon, and so on). The phases were named for the different shapes the moon seems to have. The time it takes for the moon to go through all its phases is about 29 ½ days. That time became known as a *month*, named for the moon.

Skill 3: From broad to narrow

Students are narrowing down a few subjects into usable topics: horses, the sun, and how to eat healthfully.

Skill 4: What's your main idea?

Students are narrowing down some subjects (drones and transportation) and developing possible main ideas/thesis statements for them.

Skill 5: Experienced writers

This lesson is for experienced writers. New writers can skip it.

Experienced writers are learning to develop a research topic based on a question that can be answered with a "yes" or "no," similar to a hypothesis in a science experiment. Then they are writing three such questions.

Skill 6: Paraphrasing

Students are paraphrasing Matthew 6: 9-13 (The Lord's Prayer) or Psalm 23.

Possible paraphrase for The Lord's Prayer. You students' most likely will be different:

Dear Lord, we look to you as children look to their father, and we think your name is pretty special. Please rule us and the whole earth as a king rules his kingdom. We look to you for our daily needs. We understand that you'll forgive us, but it's our job to forgive what others have done to us. Please don't be cruel and tempt us. Protect us. We owe everything to you, and you deserve our worship forever.

Possible paraphrase for Psalm 23. Your students' most likely will be different:

The Lord takes care of his people's physical, emotional, and spiritual needs like a shepherd cares for his sheep. Even when times get tough, we can count on Him to take care of us. And someday, I won't be like a sheep in a field but will be somewhere permanently—with the Lord in heaven.

Skill 7: Taking notes

Students are rearranging jumbled-up notes on three sheets of paper labeled separately as "Food," "People," and "Geography."

Food

Panamanian staples: rice, corn, legumes and beans, yams, cassava (an edible root), plantains (a kind of banana)

sancocho is rich, hearty soup made with chicken and vegetables

tamales—of cornmeal dough, stuffed with chicken, pork, or vegetables, wrapped in banana leaves and boiled

arroz con guando—rice and beans cooked in coconut milk

hojaldras—flat dough fried, sometimes with sprinkled sugar

lots of seafood

People

a "melting pot" of ethnic cultures

more than 3 million people

Native Americans

Kuna Indians in the San Blas Islands

descendants of African slaves (brought to dive for pearls years ago)

descendants of Spanish from the 1500-1800s

descendants of Chinese railroad workers

Mestizos, blend of American Indians and Spanish, most of them living in poverty

many blacks from the West Indies, Jamaica, or Barbados to work on the canal in early 1900s

many other European, East Asian, and Middle Eastern countries represented in the population

Geography

includes more than 1,500 islands

heavy rainfall, tropical

The Pacific and Caribbean coasts are at sea level.

Pacific coasts have mudflats at low tide.

Mountains run through the middle of Panama like a spine.

longest mountain range called the Cordillera Central

land bridge between Central and South America

country is 480 miles long, 30-75 miles wide

Panama shaped like an S lying down

long, narrow isthmus called the Isthmus of Panama

highest elevation—Barú Volcano at 11,401 feet

separates Pacific Ocean from the Caribbean Sea and on to the Atlantic Ocean

Skill 8: Keeping track of your sources

Teacher, if your students have never written a research report before or they are young/new writers, consider having them skip a works cited page. New or young writers should concentrate on researching and writing the report. Adding a works cited page is simply too much for them, in our opinion. The next time they write a report, *after* they have had some success in performing the skills it takes to write one, they can add a works cited page.

Students have no exercise to do in Skill 8.

However, to download a free lesson on the latest MLA (Modern Language Association) formatting and how to build a works cited page at the end of reports, go to WritingWithSharonWatson.com/jump-in/. That's where you'll find a lesson on the latest version of MLA's style.

We want to stay current with any changes MLA makes, so we are offering an up-to-date lesson on our site instead of in the textbook.

Skill 9: Organize the chaos, part 1

Students are learning two methods of organizing their ideas and notes: an outline and a list. Please go to WritingWithSharonWatson.com/outlines to download a colorful tutorial on outlining.

Students are also making an outline or a list for this topic: the dangers of writing reports. Let the humor begin!

Skill 10: Organize the chaos, part 2

Today students are using their brainstorming notes to create a cluster or a Greek temple as methods of organizing their points and material. They are also devising a main idea/thesis statement. Here's a tongue-in-cheek example:

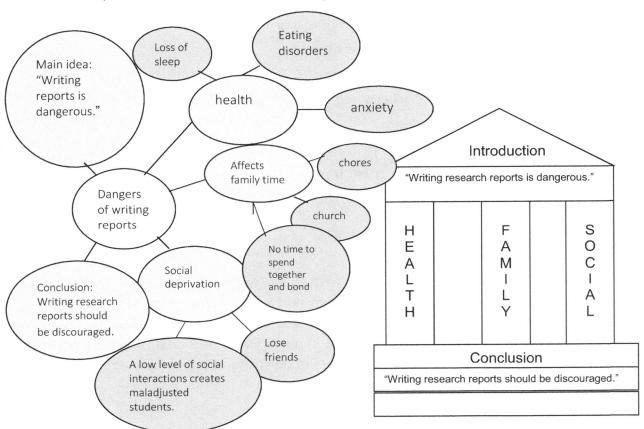

Skill 11: In-text citations

Students are taking information from sources and writing them up into in-text citations. Here are some possibilities:

"Chicken, duck, goose, pheasant—each has its own delicate taste. I would not turn up my pointed snout at any of these delicious treats," admits Dexter Foxx in *Wild Fowl I Have Known*.

According to Dexter Foxx at www.wildfowl.com, "Wild turkeys, though the hardest to run down, are the most succulent creatures for a holiday feast."

Skill 12: Vary your sentences

Students are learning to vary their sentence lengths and structures and are labeling their textbook with the number of words in each sentence and the type of sentence:

12, 3	At some point in this process, you have to begin to write. Yeah, I know. Putting words down on paper can be the most frustrating part of writing.	IP,IP (D,D)
13		D
10	Don't begin at the beginning if you don't want to. You may write the body first and the introduction and conclusion last if you like. Remember to turn off your internal editor that tells you how stupid your first sentence is. You can always go back and fix things later.	IMP
15		VV
17		
9		IMP, VV
30	If you were to gather the reports of three friends and read them, you would know which friend wrote which report, even if the names were left off the papers. How? By the way they use their words and sentences, and by the way they say things on paper. Your own style is just as distinctive. You have a certain way, a certain pattern, of writing.	IP (D)
1, 18,		I
7		F
10		D
		D

Skill 13: Topic sentence review

Students are creating topic sentences to fit written paragraphs. Here are some possibilities:

There is proof that dinosaurs and humans lived on the earth at the same time.

1) Corduroy roads were tricky, 2) Sometimes the colonists built corduroy roads, or 3) Colonial roads were of poor quality.

Skill 14: Transition sentences

Students are underlining the transition sentences in a student's report. Transition sentences:

1. When they arrived in China, they met their new commander.

2. Tex Hill was one of them.

3. Although he was such a surprisingly first-rate pilot, there were still many other great pilots.

4. Our bombers ended up smashingly knocking Japan out of the war in the skies.

And they are creating transition sentences for paragraphs from a history book. The original transition sentence for the first set of paragraphs from *First Steps in the History of Our Country* is this: "Although the land was for the most part unproductive, the waters were wonderfully full of fish." Any sentence that leads the reader from the idea of the unproductive land to abundance in the sea is acceptable.

The original transition sentence for the second set of paragraphs is this: "Why, then, should the boys and girls of the United States study the story of this almost unknown man?" Any sentence that leads the reader to wonder why we study John Cabot is acceptable.

Skill 15: Intros and conclusions review

Students evaluate the first paragraph in a chapter of a textbook of their choice. Answers will vary.

1. Was the paragraph interesting or dull? What made it so?

2. Did it include an interesting statement, fact, quotation, question, or story? If so, what?

3. What would you do to that paragraph to improve it? (No fair saying you would take it out!)

4. Based on your knowledge of how to write an introduction, what grade would you give the writer of the textbook?

Skill 16: The assignment

CHOOSE ONE:

(Use a variety of print and Web sources—at least three in any combination.)

Choose a disease, current event, or trend you are interested in. Do the research. Write a report. Include a works cited page.

Choose a country you would like someday to visit. Do the research. Write a report. Include a works cited page.

Choose a subject of interest to you. Do the research. Write a report. Include a works cited page.

Optional for experienced writers: Develop a question of the sort found in Skill 5. Research. Decide which way you lean and develop your thesis statement. Write a report. Include a works cited page.

New writers: at least 400 words. Experienced writers: at least 500 words.

A suggested writing schedule

Check off each section as you complete it:

Day 1: Decide on your topic and narrow it down. Go to the library for books and other research materials or assemble them from somewhere else.

Days 2 – 5: Plow through your research materials, take notes using the 3-ring-binder method, and make a list of your sources on the last page. Adjust your narrowed-down topic if you have to. Write your main idea (thesis statement). **Hand in your main idea** and at least three of the main points you want to make or three topic sentences.

Day 5: **Today your teacher will review your main idea and the points or topic sentences.** Make any changes your teacher suggests.

Day 6: Organize your thoughts and notes. Use an outline, list, cluster, Greek temple, or sticky notes.

Days 7-9: Write your report. Begin anywhere you wish: introductory paragraph, one of the paragraphs in the body, or the conclusion.

Day 10: Use the checklist on the next page to make sure your report is the best it can be. Make a neat copy, double-spaced (on the computer or by hand). Hand in your report *and* your method of organizing your material.

Skill 17: Use this checklist

Teacher, the grading grid for a research paper is on page 98. The student checklist is similar to your grading grid.

A Biography

Skill 1: Can you guess who these people are?

_1_ Sir James Barrie (*Peter Pan*)   _8_ Michelangelo
_5_ Beverly Cleary (*Ramona* books)   _9_ Walt Disney
_6_ Theodor Geisel (Dr. Seuss)   _3_ Helen Keller
_10_ Abraham Lincoln   _7_ Martin Luther
_4_ J. C. Penney   _2_ George Washington

1. How many of these biographies begin with the person's birth? *Only one.*

2. Why is her birth mentioned? *Because we know her as deaf, mute, and blind. It is interesting to know that she was not born that way; we are more curious about her because of the first sentence.*

3. Some of these biographies begin with a hint about how the person became famous. Why is that a good way to start a biography? *It makes us curious about the person. We may know his or her achievements, but we might not know how he or she got there.*

Skill 2: Methods you can use, part 1

Students read each method, examples, and an essay and then jot down a person who would fit those categories of biography.

Skill 3: Methods you can use, part 2

Students read each method, examples, and two essays and then jot down a person who would fit those categories of biography.

Skill 4: Don't be boring

Students list some famous people who interest them.

Skill 5: The assignment

CHOOSE ONE:

❏ Write a simple chronological biography of a famous person, living or dead. Word count: at least 300 words.

❏ Write a biography using one of the eight ways mentioned in this chapter. Word count: at least 300 words.

❏ Create a different way to write a biography and check it with your teacher. Then write the biography. Word count: at least 300 words.

Experienced writers: Your word count is at least 350 words. Use at least two sources. Also, check with your teacher to see if you are supposed to cite your sources with in-text citations and a works cited page.

A suggested writing schedule

Check off each section as you complete it:

Day 1: Decide on the person you want to write about. Go to the library or find other sources of information.

Days 2 – 5: Read your books/sources and take notes. Decide on the type of biography you want to write.

Day 6: Organize your thoughts and notes. Use an outline, list, cluster, Greek temple, or sticky notes.

Days 7-9: Write the biography.

Day 10: Proofread three separate times for mistakes and to revise anything that needs it. Use the checklist on the next page—because your teacher is. Make a neat, double-spaced copy. Hand it in.

Skill 6: Use this checklist

Teacher, the grading grid for a biography is on page 99. The student checklist is similar to your grading grid.

Compare and Contrast

Skill 1: The block method

Students are using a Venn diagram to list similarities and differences between a real Christmas tree and an artificial one. They are also writing a transition sentence from one topic to the next.

Skill 2: The feature method

Teacher, if you think your young writer is not ready for Skills 2 and 3, skip them and go to Skills 6 and 7.

1. Write the sentence that is the thesis statement in "Cats Win": *I prefer the cat.*

2. The writer of "Cats Win" focuses on three features of pets: their cleanliness, intelligence, and what else? *Politeness.*

3. Do you agree with the writer of "Cats Win"? *Personal opinion*

Skill 3: A chart for the feature method

Students are filling in a chart for the feature method on this topic: Compare and contrast Santa Claus and God.

Skill 4: Write a feature-method paragraph

Students are writing a paragraph based on the Santa Claus/God topic using the feature method.

Skill 5: Evaluate this student's essay

Students are reading and evaluating a student's essay on the differences between his two dogs.

1. Which dog does he mention first? *Winnie*

2. Which dog does he mention last? *Beau*

3. Which does he like more? *Beau*

4. What are the three features of Beau and Winnie that this student contrasts? *Kindness, the ability to do tricks, and obedience.*

5. Use one color marker or highlighter for information about Beau and one for Winnie. Does this student follow the Winnie-Beau pattern for each paragraph? *No. He mentions Beau, but he doesn't contrast him with Winnie in paragraph 2.*

7. Based on your knowledge of compare and contrast papers, what grade would you give this student? *Personal opinion; one hopes an A.*

Skill 6: The assignment

If you are a **new writer**: Choose two of something—elements of nature, people, movies, animals, or objects. Write one paragraph to compare and contrast them using the **block method**. Word count: approximately 100 words.

If you are an **experienced writer**: Choose a set of items, elements of nature, people, places, movies, or events. Write a compare-and-contrast essay using the **feature method**. Use "Cats Win" as your writing example. Word count: at least 350 words.

Suggested Writing Schedules

New writers, check off each section as you complete it:

Day 1: Decide on your set of two things. Make and fill in a Venn diagram to show similarities and differences. Decide which is more important to you—similarities or differences—and plan to put those last in your paragraph.

Day 2: Write your paragraph. To check your "blocks," mark the similarities with one color marker and the differences with another. Then proofread three separate times for mistakes and revisions. Use the checklist on the next page. Make a neat, double-spaced copy without the markers and hand it in.

Experienced writers, check off each section as you complete it:

Day 1: Decide on your set of items. List the features you want to evaluate in your essay. Research, if needed. Make a chart of features as you did in Skill 3. Decide on a point order for your features.

Days 2-3: Write the body of your paper as you would for an opinion paper. Use three separate features, which will become areas of contrast for you. Then add the contrast (differences). Use two different colored markers to highlight first the one item and then the other. Check yourself: Does each paragraph follow the same topical order (for instance, Santa Claus-then-God)? Have you avoided the Ping-Pong effect? Adjust your paragraphs as needed.

Day 4: Write the introduction and conclusion.

Day 5: Proofread three separate times for mistakes and to make the essay read more smoothly. Use the checklist on the next page. Make a neat, double-spaced copy without the highlights and hand it in.

Skill 7: Use these checklists

Teacher, you have the grading grids for compare-and-contrast paragraphs and essays on pages 100 and 101. The student checklists are similar to your grading grids.

A Book Report

Skill 1: Story elements, part 1

Students are learning about these story elements today: setting, characters, and plot. They have selected a familiar work of fiction and are answering questions about it after each element. *Answers will vary.*

What is the setting of the book?

List one main protagonist in your book. What is the main goal that pulls your protagonist through the story? How does the antagonist thwart it?

Write the plot of the book in less than 40 words.

Skill 2: Story elements, part 2

Students are learning about conflict and theme today and are using their fiction book to answer questions about those elements. *Answers will vary.*

What are your character's two main problems? Label them as "Character against."

What is one theme of your book? In other words, what might the author be trying to tell you about life?

If you were to write a book, what would you use as its theme?

Skill 3: Symbols and your opinion

Answers will vary.

What two everyday items could be used as symbols, and what could they mean?

What symbol might your author have used? What might it mean?

What is your opinion of the book? Give one or two reasons.

Skill 4: Book report form

See the complete Book Report Form on pages 18-22 in the Teacher's Guide.

Skill 5: Writing the report

Students learn what goes into each paragraph and then read a student's book report.

1. Does this student follow the suggested paragraphs? *Yes*

2. Do you think he did a good job of reporting on *Abandoned on the Wild Frontier*? *Answers will vary.*

3. Do you want to read this book? Why or why not? *Personal opinion*

Skill 6: The assignment

CHOOSE ONE:

❏ Write a book report on a favorite book. Use the Book Report Form to organize your notes. Word count: at least 300 words. Experienced writers: at least 350 words.

❏ Write a book report on a book you don't like. Use the Book Report Form to organize your notes. Word count: at least 300 words. Experienced writers: at least 350 words.

❏ Write a book report on a book your teacher assigns you. Use the Book Report Form to organize your notes. Word count: at least 300 words. Experienced writers: at least 350 words.

Book Report Planner

Tasks	Date
Read your book.	_____
Fill out the Book Report Form.	_____
Finish your first draft.	_____
Reread and revise with the checklist.	_____
Get it into its finished form.	_____
THIS IS DUE BY (Fill out this line first and work backwards from it.)	_____

Skill 7: Use this checklist

Teacher, the grading grid for a book report is on page 102. The student checklist is similar to your grading grid.

A Book Response

Skill 1: Artistic and written responses

Students are reading various ways to respond to a book other than a book report. They are also devising a new method. Teacher, you have a list of these methods on pages 23-4 in your Teacher's Guide.

Skill 2: Some examples

Students are viewing some examples of these methods.

Skill 3: The assignment

CHOOSE ONE:

❏ Decide on an artistic skill book response and complete it.

❏ Decide on a writing skill book response and complete it.

❏ Make up a new response, get it approved by your teacher, and complete it.

Book Response Schedule

<u>Task</u>   <u>Date</u> ___

Read a book.
Decide on a book response.   _____
Finish your first draft (if necessary).   _____
Reread and revise (if necessary).   _____
Put your response into its finished form.   _____
THIS IS DUE BY   (Fill out this line first   _____
                and work backwards from it.)

Teacher, the grading grid for a book response is on page 103. Students have no checklist for this assignment.

Description

Skill 1: One word

Students are choosing specific nouns, adjectives, and verbs to describe items and motion.

Skill 2: Make a boring paragraph sparkle

Answers will vary. Here is one example (167 words):

   My sister Beth and I glanced out the kitchen window and saw a swirling, black tornado rushing toward us! We grabbed our little brother Marcos and ran to our old, beat-up Chevy truck. Beth pulled the door open, and we jumped in. Our plan was to outrun the tornado. All of us were so frightened, especially when we remembered that it's foolish to try to outrun a tornado. I decided we should hide in a closet under the stairs, so we pulled Marcos from the truck, ran to the house, and jammed ourselves into the tiny closet. Beth slammed the door closed and shut us in. I could feel all of us shivering from fright. Then we heard that awful train sound. I heard the house moan and felt it vibrate around me. Suddenly, there was complete silence. Beth and I peeked out of the closet and stared at what was left of our house. The kitchen was gone! Now I won't have to wash the dishes!

Check off each day as you complete it:

Day 1: Rewrite the paragraph. Use vivid and specific verbs, nouns, and adjectives. Avoid adverbs (words that end in –ly, like "hurriedly," "happily," "menacingly," and so on).

Day 2: Proofread three times using the checklist on the next page. Make a neat, double-spaced copy.

Teacher, the grading grid for this assignment is on page 104. The student checklist is similar to your grading grid.

Skill 3: Simile and metaphor

Students are writing similes and identifying metaphors.

Skill 4: Use your senses.

Students are finding a place to sit and record sensory information for ten minutes.

Skill 5: Describe a room

Students are reading a sample description, answering the following questions about it, and writing their own description of a room.

1. Which sense does he use the most? *Hearing, which is appropriate for an orchestra room.*

2. What other senses does he use? *Seeing, feeling*

3. Underline his two similes. *I can feel my body shivering like a cat in the strong wind…, …hop into the van like a kangaroo.*

4. Put an X next to his metaphor. *Mrs. Goldman is a ballerina dancing on the conducting platform.*

Check off each section as you complete it:

Day 1: Decide on a real or imaginary place. Using your descriptive skills—including senses—and write about it. Avoid adverbs.

Day 2: Proofread three times with the checklist below. Make a neat, double-spaced copy.

Teacher, the grading grid for this assignment is on page 105. The student checklist is similar to your grading grid.

Skill 6: Spatial description

1. What do you think she heard in the forest? *Personal opinion and imagination*

2. What direction is the spatial description? *Head to knees*

3. Underline her simile. *…like twin vines…*

4. **Assonance** is repeating a vowel sound on the insides of words in a row. Edgar Allan Poe uses assonance in his poem "The Bells": "m**o**lten-g**o**lden n**o**tes." Where does the writer of this paragraph use assonance? *H**u**ng, sw**u**ng*

Check off each day as you complete it:

Day 1: Describe a character or real person. Use all of your descriptive skills plus a spatial description.

Day 2: Proofread three times with the checklist below. Make a neat, double-spaced copy.

Teacher, the grading grid for this assignment is on page 106. The student checklist is similar to your grading grid.

Skill 7: Movement

1. What is the direction of the spatial description? *Top to bottom (from the canopy of the trees to the ground)*

2. What is moving? *Milo and his friends run. The sunlight leaped, slid, and dropped.*

3. Would you like to be in that place with Milo? Explain. *Personal opinion*

4. **Alliteration** is a series of words beginning with the same sound. Edgar Allan Poe uses alliteration in his poem "The Bells": "What a <u>t</u>ale of <u>t</u>error, now their <u>t</u>urbulency <u>t</u>ells!" Where is the alliteration in this paragraph about Milo and the woods? *<u>L</u>eaped <u>l</u>ightly from <u>l</u>eaf to <u>l</u>eaf*

Check off each day as you complete it:

Day 1: Describe a scene from life or invented. Use all of your descriptive skills and make something *move*.

Day 2: Proofread three times with the checklist below. Make a neat, double-spaced copy.

Teacher, the grading grid for this assignment is on page 107. The student checklist is similar to your grading grid.

Skill 8: Create a mood

In one paragraph, describe what the cottage looks like to Hansel and Gretel when they first glimpse it in the woods: most likely inviting and welcoming.

In another paragraph, describe what the cottage looks like to the children as they look back while fleeing it: perhaps dark and frightening.

Check off each day as you complete it:

Day 1: Write your lists for each mood you want to create: light and inviting versus dark and frightening.

Day 2: Use your lists to write one paragraph for each mood. Use all of your descriptive skills.

Day 3: Proofread each paragraph three times with the checklist below. Make a neat, double-spaced copy.

Alternate schedule

Check off each day as you complete it:

Day 1: Write a list for one of the moods you want to create and then write your paragraph.

Day 2: Write a list for the other mood you want to create and then write the second paragraph.

Day 3: Proofread each paragraph three times with the checklist below. Make a neat, double-spaced copy.

Teacher, the grading grid for this assignment is on page 108. The student checklist is similar to your grading grid.

Teacher, my classes have had loads of fun with this activity: Create two teams. One will work with the light mood; the other, the dark. Have each team make lists of items, colors, and so on, for their particular mood and then write the paragraph. At the end of an allotted time, have each team read their paragraph to the other team.

Narration

Skill 1: Your own story

Students are learning personal narration guidelines and reading an example. Answers to the following questions will vary. One hopes students will mark mostly 5s.

_____ How well did the writer **set the scene**?

_____ How well did her **descriptions** help you see what was going on?

_____ How well did she tell her story **chronologically**?

_____ How well did her **dialog** help the story?

_____ How well did her **reactions** to the events in the story help you understand how she felt and also give meaning to the events?

_____ How well did she avoid "teaching" you but write what the story **means to her**?

Overall grade: _____

Check off each day as you complete it:

Day 1: Throw around some ideas of a personal story you could write about. Decide on one of them. Get any additional facts you may need.

Day 2: Write your personal narrative.

Day 3: Read the list of personal narrative guidelines and add in any elements that will make it stronger.

Day 4: Proofread three times with the checklist on the next page. Make a neat, double-spaced copy.

Teacher, the grading grid for as personal narrative is on page 109. The student checklist is similar to your grading grid.

Skill 2: Hooks

1. There once was a boy named Milo who didn't know what to do with himself—not just sometimes, but always. (*The Phantom Tollbooth* by Norton Juster)

2. It was a dull autumn day and Pole was crying behind the gym. (*The Silver Chair* by C. S. Lewis)

3. Marley was dead: to begin with. (*A Christmas Carol* by Charles Dickens)

4. All children, except one, grow up. (*Peter Pan* by Sir James Barrie)

5. There was once upon a time...

   "A king!" my little readers will instantly exclaim.

   No, children, you are wrong. There was once upon a time a piece of wood. (*Pinocchio* by C. Collodi)

6. "Where's Papa going with that ax?" said Fern to her mother as they were setting the table for breakfast. (*Charlotte's Web* by E. B. White)

Students are writing their own hooks. It can be especially fun to do this as a group, exchange hooks, and write from another's hook.

Days 1-2: Write the hooks. Find the friends, exchange the hooks, and write a story from a hook. Write for 10 minutes. No need to proofread. Have fun!

Skill 3: Character trait

Check off each section as you complete it:

Days 1-3: Choose or invent a character. Make a list of ways to show readers one particular trait of this character. Then write the situation to show your character's trait.

Day 4: Proofread three times using the checklist below. Make a neat, double-spaced copy. For a bit of fun, read your scene to someone to see if they can guess the trait you are trying to portray.

Teacher, the grading grid for this assignment is on page 110. The student checklist is similar to your grading grid.

Teacher, one fun activity with this lesson is to have students write the scenes for their character traits and then read them aloud to see if other students can guess the trait they are trying to portray.

Skill 4: Point of view

3 1. His children, too, were as ragged and wild as if they belonged to nobody. His son Rip, an urchin begotten in his own likeness, promised to inherit the habits, with the old clothes, of his father. ("Rip Van Winkle" by Washington Irving)

1 2. For <u>my</u> part, <u>I</u> cannot say that <u>my</u> reflections were very agreeable. <u>I</u> knew that <u>we</u> were on an island, for Jack had said so, but whether it was inhabited or not <u>I</u> did not know. (*The Coral Island* by R. M. Ballantyne)

1 3. After darkly looking at his leg and at <u>me</u> several times, he came closer to <u>my</u> tombstone, took <u>me</u> by both arms, and tilted <u>me</u> back as far as he could hold <u>me</u>; so that his eyes looked most powerfully down into <u>mine</u>, and <u>mine</u> looked most helplessly up into his. (*Great Expectations* by Charles Dickens)

3 4. The wanderings of the tribe brought them often near the closed and silent cabin by the little land-locked harbor. To Tarzan this was always a source of never-ending mystery and pleasure. (*Tarzan of the Apes* by Edgar Rice Burroughs)

3 5. She had been lying awake turning from side to side for about an hour, when suddenly something made her sit up in bed and turn her head toward the door listening. She listened and she listened. (*The Secret Garden* by Frances Hodgson Burnett)

3 6. His sobs woke Wendy, and she sat up in bed. She was not alarmed to see a stranger crying on the nursery floor; she was only pleasantly interested. (*Peter Pan* by Sir James Barrie)

1 7. You may fancy the terror <u>I</u> was in! <u>I</u> should have leaped out and run for it, if <u>I</u> had found the strength; but <u>my</u> limbs and heart alike misgave <u>me</u>. (*Treasure Island* by Robert Louis Stevenson)

1 8. But the next event to be related is terrible indeed. Its very memory, even now, makes <u>my</u> soul shudder and <u>my</u> blood run cold. (*Journey to the Center of the Earth* by Jules Verne)

1 9. The noise at night would have been annoying to <u>me</u> ordinarily, but <u>I</u> didn't mind it in the present circumstances, because it kept <u>me</u> from hearing the quacks detaching legs and arms from the day's cripples. (*A Connecticut Yankee in King Arthur's Court* by Mark Twain)

3 10. Two of the strongest monkeys caught Mowgli under the arms and swung off with him through the tree-tops, twenty feet at a bound. (*The Jungle Book* by Rudyard Kipling)

Skill 5: Point of view again

Answer to the Jonah question in the text: *third person*

Check off each section as you complete it:

Days 1-3: Read Daniel 2. Choose an existing person from the chapter or invent a character. Choose the point of view. Write the story.

Day 4: Proofread three times with the checklist below. Make a neat, double-spaced copy.

Teacher, the grading grid for this assignment is on page 111. The student checklist is similar to your grading grid.

Skill 6: Motivation

Students are devising reasons (motivations) why children and teens can't go to the adults in the story, other than the adults are stupid, mean, clueless, and so on.

Skill 7: Resolve a conflict

Check off each section as you complete it:

Days 1-3: Write the story. Resolve the conflict.

Day 4: Proofread three times with the checklist on the next page. Make a neat, double-spaced copy.

Teacher, the grading grid for this assignment is on page 112. The student checklist is similar to your grading grid.

Skill 8: Dialog

1. What does the dialogue tell you about the plot? *There is trouble brewing between England and Scotland.*

2. What does the dialogue tell you about the characters? *Duncan is brother to the man and is a Scotsman; the man and his wife are religious; the human girl thinks the dwarf is ugly.*

3. What POV is it written in? *First person*

4. From whose perspective is it written? *From the perspective of the dwarf*

5. Is there a good balance between dialogue and narration? *Yes; student opinion.*

Skill 9: Dialog punctuation and narrative action

Students are writing a conversation between two people who are stuck on an elevator.

Check off each section as you complete it:

Days 1-2: Write the dialogue and some narrative actions.

Day 3: Check and correct the dialogue punctuation and paragraphs.

Day 4: Proofread three times with the checklist. Make a neat, double-spaced copy.

Teacher, the grading grid for this assignment is on page 113. The student checklist is similar to your grading grid.

Skill 10: Fables and morals

Moral: *Answers will vary. One possible moral: Never attend a picnic with a fox, especially if you are a chicken. OR Do not trust an enemy, even if he seems friendly.*

Check off each section as you complete it:

Day 1: Choose or invent a moral, saying, or proverb. Brainstorm possible stories.

Days 2-3: Write the fable to demonstrate the moral. Use animals, if appropriate. Include the moral at the end of your fable.

Day 4: Proofread three times with the checklist below. Make a neat, double-spaced copy.

Teacher, the grading grid for this assignment is on page 114. The student checklist is similar to your grading grid.

Skill 11: Patterns of three

Patterns of 3 in the fable in Skill 10*: (1) three chickens with names all beginning with the letter R, (2) fox throws the Frisbee three times, (3) chickens retrieve it three times, (4) fox digs three holes.*

Students are listing patterns of three they find in life, literature, the Bible, and so on. *Answers will vary.*

Skill 12: Fairy tale, tall tale, Just So story, and parable

Pattern of three: *Three animals—the buck, the rabbit, and the squirrel, each animal a size smaller*

Check off each section as you complete it:

Day 1: Read some fairy tales, tall tales, and so forth, to get ideas.

Days 2-4: Write a fairy tale, tall tale, Just So story, or parable. Include a pattern of three.

Day 5: Proofread three times using the checklist below. Make a neat, double-spaced copy.

Teacher, the grading grid for this assignment is on page 115. The student checklist is similar to your grading grid.

Skill 13: Story ideas

Students are reading story ideas and adding some of their own to the list.

Poetry

Teacher, there are no grading grids for the poetry chapter.

Skill 1: Haiku

Students are writing a haiku. Answers will vary.

Skill 2: Cinquain

Students are writing a cinquain. Answers will vary.

Skill 3: Diamante

Students are writing a diamante. Answers will vary.

Skill 4: Limericks

Students are writing a limerick. Answers will vary.

Skill 5: Hymns

Students are writing a new hymn. Answers will vary.

My Jesus, I love Thee, I know Thou art mine.	___A___
For Thee all the follies of sin I resign.	___A___
My gracious Redeemer, my Savior art Thou.	___B___
If ever I loved Thee, my Jesus, 'tis now.	___B___

OR

My Jesus, I love Thee, I know Thou art mine.	___A___
For Thee all the follies of sin I resign.	___A___
My gracious Redeemer, my Savior art Thou.	___B___
If ever I loved Thee, my Jesus, 'tis now.	___B___

Amazing grace! How sweet the sound	___A___
That saved a wretch like me!	___B___
I once was lost but now am found,	___A___
Was blind but now I see.	___B___

Skill 6: Imitate a poem

Students are imitating the rhythm and rhyme scheme of a poem of their choice.

Skill 7: Write new lyrics

Students are writing new lyrics to an existing song.

Grading Grids

Opinion Essay

STUDENT
NAME_____

	Comments:
Has the student communicated his/her ideas clearly and expressed them well? 1-10 points	
Is there something noteworthy about the ideas or the writing (humor, insightfulness, obvious delight for the topic, and so on)? 1-10 points	
Does the opening sentence or paragraph grab the reader's attention? 1-5 points	
Does the introduction clearly introduce the topic and opinion? 1-10 points	
Are there 3 points? Are they solid? Do they support the opinion well? 1-20 points	
Are they arranged in an effective order? 1-5 points	
Are there topic sentences for each point? Does each paragraph support its topic sentence well? 1-20 points	
Does the conclusion adequately sum up the topic and opinion? 1-5 points	
Are there separate paragraphs for the intro, each point, and conclusion? 1-5 pts.	
Was the paper handed in on time? 1-10 points	
Grade	

Note: Students will express their opinion in the introduction; however, they have not yet learned about thesis statements. Also, grammar and mechanics are not graded in this first essay of the year.

Writing with Sharon Watson

Persuasive Essay

STUDENT
NAME_____

Is each point devised to convince readers to change their thinking and/or behavior? 1-10 points ◯

Does the opening sentence or paragraph grab the reader's attention? 1-5 points ◯

Does the introduction clearly introduce the topic and view? 1-10 points ◯

Has the student communicated his/her ideas clearly and expressed them well? 1-15 points ◯

Has the student avoided everything on the Don't List and included strategies from the Do List (Skill 10 in "Persuasion: The Basics")? 1-10 points ◯

Are the topic sentences clear? Do the paragraphs support the topic sentences? 1-15 points ◯

Are there 3 points? Are they solid? Are they arranged in an effective order? 1-15 points ◯

Does the conclusion issue a specific and measurable call to action? 1-5 points ◯

Does the conclusion adequately sum up the topic and view, giving food for thought? 1-5 points ◯

Is there something noteworthy about the ideas or the writing (humor, insightfulness, and so on)? 1-10 points ◯

Extra credit: Does the essay refute an argument? 10 points ◯

Grade for Content ◯

Comments:

How are the spelling, capitalization, punctuation, fragments, run-on sentences, and so on? 1-25 points ◯

Are there separate paragraphs for the intro, each point, and conclusion? 1-25 points ◯

Was the paper handed in on time? 1-25 points ◯

Did the student follow the written instructions? 1-25 points ◯

Grade for Grammar/Mechanics ◯

Writing with Sharon Watson

Cause-and-Effect Persuasive Essay

STUDENT

NAME_____

Comments:

Is each point devised to convince readers to change their thinking and/or behavior, and is each solid? 1-15 points	◯
Is the introduction intriguing? Does it include the inventor, time period, and short history of the invention, if necessary? 1-10 points	◯
Does the introduction clearly introduce the topic and view? 1-10 points	◯
Has the student communicated his/her ideas clearly and expressed them well? 1-15 points	◯
Is the link between the cause and the effects clear? (Basically, "Because of *that*, all of *this* has happened.") 1-10 points	◯
Does each paragraph have a solid topic sentence and clear supporting statements? 1-15 points	◯
Are the paragraphs arranged in an effective order? 1-5 points	◯
Does the conclusion issue a specific and measurable call to action? 1-5 points	◯
Does the conclusion adequately sum up the topic and view, giving food for thought? 1-5 points	◯
Does the essay choose a side and stick to all negative effects or all positive ones? 1-10 points	◯
Extra credit: Is there something noteworthy about the ideas or the writing (humor, insightfulness, and so on)? 1-10 points	◯
Grade for Content	◯

How are the spelling, capitalization, punctuation, fragments, run-on sentences, and so on? 1-25 points	◯
Are there separate paragraphs for the intro, each point, and conclusion? 1-25 points	◯
Was the paper handed in on time? 1-25 points	◯
Did the student follow the written instructions? 1-25 points	◯
Grade for Grammar/Mechanics	◯

Newspaper Article

STUDENT
NAME_____

Comments:

Does the student adequately report the event? 1-20 points	◯
Does the lead include the appropriate Ws and the H (who, what, when, where, why, and how)? 1-10 points	◯
Is the sentence that sums up the significance concise and does it convey the importance of the event? 1-10 points	◯
Are the following paragraphs in the inverted pyramid order (most important to least important)? 1-15 points	◯
Does the student use facts and avoid opinions (except in quotes)? 1-10 points	◯
Is the article interesting, clear, and concise? Is the event told chronologically? 1-15 pts	◯
Are the quotes, if any, appropriate to the story? 1-10 points	◯
Are the quotes and facts correctly attributed or cited? 1-10 points	◯
Extra credit: Is the article insightful or otherwise noteworthy? 1-10 points	◯
Grade for Content	◯

Are the paragraphs short? Are the sentences simple? 1-20 points	◯
Are the article and attributions in the past tense? 1-20 points	◯
How are the spelling, capitalization, punctuation, sentence fragments, run-ons, and so on? 1-20 points	◯
Was the paper handed in on time? 1-20 points	◯
Did the student follow the written instructions? 1-20 points	◯
Grade for Grammar/Mechanics	◯

How-to Instruction-Manual Method

STUDENT
NAME_____

Comments:

Is the list clear, complete, and chronological? 1-50 points

Are the items or ingredients listed? 1-5 pts. If no list is needed, give 5 points anyway.

If transitions are needed, are they included? 1-5 points

Does each item in the list begin with an imperative verb in the present tense? 1-10 pts

If a chart is needed, is it present, helpful, and clear? 1-5 points. If no chart is needed, give 5 points anyway.

Is the jargon well defined? 1-5 points

Is it clear that the instructions are geared for particular audience? 1-10 points

Did the student write the intended audience on his/her paper? 1-10 points

Extra credit: Is there something noteworthy or insightful about the paper or the writing (humor, clarity, tone, and so on)? 1-10 points

Grade for Content

How are the spelling, capitalization, punctuation, sentence fragments, run-ons, and so on? 1-25 points

Was the paper handed in on time? 1-25 points

Did the student follow the written instructions? 1-25 points

Grade for Grammar/Mechanics

How-to Essay

STUDENT
NAME_____

Comments:

Does the introduction set the tone and clearly tell readers what is being taught? 1-10 points	
Is there a list of needed items or ingredients, if necessary? 1-5 points. If no list is needed, give 5 points anyway.	
Are the steps chronological, clear, and complete? 1-15 points	
Do the transitions move the reader along easily from step to step? 1-10 points	
If a chart is needed, is it present, helpful, and clear? 1-5 points. If no chart is needed, give 5 points anyway.	
Is the jargon well defined? 1-10 points	
Does the conclusion adequately sum up the topic, maybe encouraging readers to try it? 1-10 points	
Is it clear that the paper is focused on a particular audience (age, gender, and so on)? 1-10 points	
Does the paper adequately describe the process? Are the ideas expressed well? 1-25 points	
Extra credit: Is there something noteworthy or insightful about the paper or the writing (humor, clarity, tone, and so on)? 1-10 points	
Grade for Content	

How are the spelling, capitalization, punctuation, sentence fragments, run-ons, and so on? 1-25 points	
Are there separate paragraphs for the intro, the steps, and the conclusion? 1-25 points	
Was the paper handed in on time? 1-25 points	
Did the student follow the written instructions? 1-25 points	
Grade for Grammar/Mechanics	

Research Report

STUDENT
NAME_____

Is the topic interesting and has it been narrowed down to a manageable size? 1-10 points	○
Do the title and introduction interest the reader? 1-5 points	○
Is the main idea (thesis statement) clear? Is it near the end of the first paragraph? 1-10 points	○
Is each point strong? Does each support the main idea? Are the ideas clearly expressed and of value? 1-20 points	○
Does the student cite all borrowed facts, ideas, quotations, and so on? 1-10 points	○
Does each point have a clear topic sentence? Do the paragraphs adequately support the topic sentences? 1-15 points	○
Are the paragraphs arranged in an effective order? Are there transitions between the paragraphs? 1-5 pts	○
Does the conclusion restate or sum up the main idea in a new way and give food for thought? 1-5 points	○
Is it clear that the student organized his/her material before writing? Did the student hand in his/her organizing tool? 1-10 points	○
Is it clear that the research was done well? 1-10 points	○
Extra credit: Is there something noteworthy in the writing, the expression of ideas, or in the research? 1-10 points	○
Grade for Content	○

Comments:

Are in-text citations correct and used where needed? Is the works cited page correct? 1-20 points	○
How are the spelling, capitalization, punctuation, sentence fragments, run-ons, and so on? 1-20 points	○
Are there separate paragraphs for the intro, each point, and conclusion? 1-20 points	○
Was the paper handed in on time? 1-20 points	○
Did the student follow the written instructions? 1-20 points	○
Grade for Grammar/Mechanics	○

Writing with Sharon Watson

Biography

STUDENT
NAME_____

Comments:

Is the biography interesting to read? Does it answer any questions it puts in the reader's mind? 1-25 points	
Does the biography cover the person's life, slice of life, or trait well? 1-25 points	
Does the introduction capture the reader's attention? 1-10 points	
Are there at least two transitions from paragraph to paragraph? 1-10 points	
Is the research from at least two credible sources? 1-15 points	
Is the tale told chronologically or in another manner that makes sense? 1-15 points	
Extra credit: Is the biography insightful or otherwise noteworthy? 1-10 points	
Grade for Content	

How are the spelling, capitalization, punctuation, sentence fragments, run-ons, and so on? 1-25 points	
Is there an introduction and a conclusion? Does the internal paragraphing make sense? 1-25 points	
Was the paper handed in on time? 1-25 points	
Did the student follow the written instructions? 1-25 points	
Extra credit for older students: Is the source material documented correctly with in-text citations, parenthetical notations and a works cited page? 1-10 points	
Grade for Grammar/Mechanics	

Writing with Sharon Watson

Compare-and-Contrast Paragraph in the Block Method

STUDENT
NAME_____

Comments:

Did the student make a Venn diagram of similarities and differences? 1-15 points	⬭
Do the two chosen items make sense when examined together? 1-15 points	⬭
Does the student write about his or her more important item last? 1-15 points	⬭
Is there a transition from one section to the next? 1-5 points	⬭
Are the ideas well expressed? 1-40 points	⬭
Did the student use two different-colored markers to highlight similarities and differences? 1-10 points	⬭
Extra credit: Is the paragraph insightful or otherwise noteworthy? 1-10 points	⬭
Grade for Content	⬭

How are the spelling, capitalization, punctuation, sentence fragments, run-ons, and so on? 1-25 points	⬭
Does the organization of material make sense concerning the two topics being compared and contrasted? 1-25 pts	⬭
Was the paper handed in on time? 1-25 points	⬭
Did the student follow the written instructions? 1-25 points	⬭
Grade for Grammar/Mechanics	⬭

Writing with
Sharon Watson

Compare-and-Contrast Essay in the Feature Method

STUDENT
NAME_____

Comments:

Did the student make a chart of features? 1-10 points	◯
Do the two items, people, places, events, and so on, make sense when examined together? 1-10 points	◯
Does the introduction capture the reader's attention and show or hint at the two topics being examined? 1-10 points	◯
Is the internal structure of each feature orderly? For instance, cat-then-dog, cat-then-dog, cat-then-dog. 1-10 points	◯
Are there transitions from one feature to the next? 1-5 points	◯
Is it clear that the student prefers one item or person over the other, if that is appropriate to the topic? 1-10 points	◯
Are the ideas well expressed? Does the student express something insightful or helpful about the chosen items? 1-35 points	◯
Does the conclusion sum up the topics? Does it draw a conclusion or make an insightful judgment about the two topics being examined? 1-10 points	◯
Extra credit: Is the essay insightful or otherwise noteworthy? 1-10 points	◯
Grade for Content	◯

Does the organization of material make sense concerning the two topics being compared and contrasted? 1-25 points	◯
How are the spelling, capitalization, punctuation, sentence fragments, run-ons, and so on? 1-25 points	◯
Was the paper handed in on time? 1-25 points	◯
Did the student follow the written instructions? 1-25 points	◯
Grade for Grammar/Mechanics	◯

Writing with Sharon Watson

Book Report

STUDENT
NAME_____

Comments:

Are the name of the book and the author in the first paragraph? 1-5 points

Does the introduction capture the reader's interest? 1-5 points

Is the setting (time and place) of the book briefly mentioned? 1-5 points

Are the main character's biggest problems or longings mentioned clearly? 1-15 points

Does the student concisely sum up the plot, showing how exciting or interesting the book is? 1-15 points

Are there examples and quotations from the book to prove the student's conception of the theme? 1-15 points

If needed, is there a brief author biography using any facts that relate to the theme or why the author wrote the book? 1-5 pts

Does the report include examples of special features of the story such as plot twists, figurative language, symbols, and so on? 1-10 pts

Does the student express an opinion of the book, citing its strengths and/or weaknesses? 1-15 points

Does the student include what he or she learned from the book? 1-10 points

Extra credit: Is there something noteworthy in the writing, the expression of ideas, or in the research? 1-10 points

Grade
for Content

Does the report follow the Book Report Form? 1-20 points

How are the spelling, capitalization, punctuation, sentence fragments, run-ons, and so on? 1-20 points

Are there separate paragraphs for the intro, each point, and conclusion? 1-20 points

Was the paper handed in on time? 1-20 points

Did the student follow the written instructions? 1-20 points

Grade
for Grammar/Mechanics

Writing with
Sharon Watson

Book Response

STUDENT
NAME_____

Comments:

Does the project show some competence in the method the student chose (skill in painting for instance)? 1-20 points	◯
Does the project show or highlight something of interest in the book? 1-20 pts	◯
Is the book response appropriate to the story, its themes, or its author? 1-20 pts	◯
Does the project reflect the amount of time and effort you wanted the student to spend on it? 1-20 points	◯
Did the student hand in the project on time? 1-20 points	◯
Extra credit: Is there something noteworthy about the project or the student's work on it? 1-10 points	◯
Grade	◯

Writing with Sharon Watson

Description: Make a boring paragraph sparkle

STUDENT
NAME_____

(Students are rewriting a lackluster paragraph about a tornado. They are using specific nouns and adjectives and vivid verbs to capture the reader's interest.)

Comments:

Does the new paragraph rely on powerful, vivid verbs? 1-25 points	◯
Are the adjectives and nouns specific? Did the student avoid most adverbs? 1-25 points	◯
Has the student made the boring paragraph compelling? 1-25 points	◯
Did it hold your interest? 1-25 points	◯
Extra credit: Is the new paragraph insightful or otherwise noteworthy? 1-10 points	◯
Grade for Content	◯

How are the spelling, capitalization, punctuation, sentence fragments, run-ons, and so on? 1-30 points	◯
Was the paper handed in on time? 1-35 points	◯
Did the student follow the written instructions? 1-35 points	◯
Grade for Grammar/Mechanics	◯

Writing with Sharon Watson

Describe a Room

STUDENT
NAME_____

(Students are writing to describe a real or imaginary room.)

Comments:

By reading the description, can you clearly see the room in your mind? 1-20 points ◯

Does the student use powerful, vivid verbs? 1-20 points ◯

Does the student use one simile or metaphor? 1-10 points ◯

Does the description include sensory information (sight, sound, touch, and so on) that shows how the student feels about the room? 1-20 points ◯

Are the adjectives and nouns specific? 1-15 points ◯

Did you enjoy reading the description? 1-15 points ◯

Extra credit: Is the description insightful or otherwise noteworthy? 1-10 points ◯

Grade for Content ◯

How are the spelling, capitalization, punctuation, sentence fragments, run-ons, and so on? 1-30 points ◯

Was the paper handed in on time? 1-35 points ◯

Did the student follow the written instructions? 1-35 points ◯

Grade for Grammar/Mechanics ◯

Writing with
Sharon Watson

Describe a Character or Person

STUDENT
NAME_____

Comments:

By reading the description, can you clearly see the person in your mind? 1-20 points	◯
Does the student use a spatial description (head to foot, left to right, and so on)? 1-10 points	◯
Does the student use powerful, vivid verbs? 1-15 points	◯
Does the student use one simile or metaphor? 1-10 points	◯
Does the description include sensory information (sight, sound, touch, and so on) that add to how the student wants readers to react to this person? 1-20 pts	◯

Are the adjectives and nouns specific? 1-10 points	◯	How are the spelling, capitalization, punctuation, sentence fragments, run-ons, and so on? 1-30 points	◯
Did you enjoy reading the description? 1-15 points	◯	Was the paper handed in on time? 1-35 points	◯
Extra credit: Is the description insightful or otherwise noteworthy? 1-10 points	◯	Did the student follow the written instructions? 1-35 points	◯
Grade for Content	◯	Grade for Grammar/Mechanics	◯

Writing with
Sharon Watson

Describe a Scene

STUDENT
NAME_____

(Students are describing a scene: fairgrounds, doctor's office, teams practicing for a game, and so on.)

Comments:

By reading the scene, can you clearly see it in your mind? 1-20 points ◯

Does the student make something move? 1-10 points ◯

Does the student use a spatial description (head to foot, left to right, and so on)? 1-10 points ◯

Does the student use powerful, vivid verbs? 1-15 points ◯

Does the student use one simile or metaphor? 1-10 points ◯

Does the description include sensory information (sight, sound, touch, and so on) that gives readers a feel for the scene? 1-15 points ◯

Are the adjectives and nouns specific? 1-10 points ◯

Did you enjoy reading the scene? 1-10 points ◯

Extra credit: Is the description insightful or otherwise noteworthy? 1-10 points ◯

Grade for Content ◯

How are the spelling, capitalization, punctuation, sentence fragments, run-ons, and so on? 1-30 points ◯

Was the paper handed in on time? 1-35 points ◯

Did the student follow the written instructions? 1-35 points ◯

Grade for Grammar/Mechanics ◯

Writing with Sharon Watson

Create a Mood

STUDENT
NAME_____

(Students are writing two separate paragraphs: one for when Hansel and Gretel first see the cottage—a light and inviting mood—and one for when the children flee the witch and cottage—a dark and frightening mood.)

Comments:

By reading the two paragraphs, can you clearly guess each mood created? 1-20 pts ◯

Does the student make something move? 1-10 points ◯

Does the student use a spatial description (close to far, left to right, and so on)? 1-10 points ◯

Does the student use powerful, vivid verbs that add to the mood? 1-15 points ◯

Does the student use one simile or metaphor that reflects the mood? 1-10 pts ◯

Does the description include sensory information (sight, sound, touch, and so on) that gives readers a feel for each scene? 1-15 points ◯

Are the adjectives and nouns specific? 1-10 points ◯

How are the spelling, capitalization, punctuation, sentence fragments, run-ons, and so on? 1-30 points ◯

Did you enjoy reading the paragraphs? 1-10 points ◯

Was the paper handed in on time? 1-35 points ◯

Extra credit: Is the description insightful or otherwise noteworthy? 1-10 points ◯

Did the student follow the written instructions? 1-35 points ◯

Grade for Content ◯

Grade for Grammar/Mechanics ◯

Writing with Sharon Watson

Personal Narrative

STUDENT
NAME_____

Comments:

Is the scene set by including a time frame (winter, in the morning, last year, and so on) and location? 1-10 points

Did the student include short descriptions of people, places, or items? 1-15 points

Did the student tell the story chronologically? 1-25 points

If dialog is used, does it help the narrative along? 1-10 points

Does the narrative include sensory information (sight, sound, touch, and so on), movement, a spatial description, or figurative language? 1-15

Did the student include personal reactions or the reactions of others to events in the story? 1-10 points

Did the student avoid "teaching" readers? Does the narrative show what the student learned or how the student was changed? 1-15 points

Extra credit: Is the story insightful or otherwise noteworthy? 1-10 points

Grade for Content

How are the spelling, capitalization, punctuation, sentence fragments, run-ons, and so on? 1-30 points

Was the paper handed in on time? 1-35 points

Did the student follow the written instructions? 1-35 points

Grade for Grammar/Mechanics

Writing with Sharon Watson

Character Trait

STUDENT
NAME_____

Comments:

Is the character "acting out" the trait naturally in the scene? 1-30 points	◯
Do the student's clues point to the trait he/she is aiming for? 1-25 points	◯
Can you guess correctly what trait the student is trying to show? 1-10 points	◯
Does the student avoid mentioning the trait or its synonyms in the story (like *friendly*, *grumpy*, or *greedy*)? 1-20 pts	◯
Did you enjoy reading about the character in this situation? 1-15 points	◯
Extra credit: Is the situation insightful or otherwise noteworthy? 1-10 points	◯
Grade for Content	◯

How are the spelling, capitalization, punctuation, sentence fragments, run-ons, and so on? 1-30 points	◯
Was the paper handed in on time? 1-35 points	◯
Did the student follow the written instructions? 1-35 points	◯
Grade for Grammar/Mechanics	◯

Writing with
Sharon Watson

Point of View

STUDENT
NAME_____

Comments:

Did the student adequately rewrite an existi~~ng~~
Bible account or fairy tale? 1-30 points ◯

Did the student choose one historical
person or character to be the new main
character? 1-20 points ◯

Is the point of view consistent throughout
the story (always first or third person, for
instance)? 1-30 points ◯

Did you enjoy reading the story?
1-20 points ◯

Extra credit: Is the story insightful
or otherwise noteworthy? 1-10 points ◯

Grade
for Content ◯

How are the spelling, capitalization,
punctuation, sentence fragments,
run-ons, and so on? 1-30 points ◯

Was the paper handed in on time?
1-35 points ◯

Did the student follow the written
instructions? 1-35 points ◯

Grade
for Grammar/Mechanics ◯

Writing with Sharon Watson

Resolve a Conflict

STUDENT
NAME_____

(Students are writing from a prompt about two friends who suddenly are in trouble.)

Comments:

Does the story show how much trouble the two friends are in and that it is serious? 1-20 points ◯

Does the student let the problem get worse before it is resolved? 1-20 points ◯

Does the story show how hard this conflict is on both friends? 1-20 points ◯

Do you appreciate the way the conflict was resolved? 1-20 points ◯

Did you enjoy reading the story? 1-20 points ◯

Extra credit: Is the story insightful or otherwise noteworthy? 1-10 points ◯

Grade for Content ◯

How are the spelling, capitalization, punctuation, sentence fragments, run-ons, and so on? 1-30 points ◯

Was the paper handed in on time? 1-35 points ◯

Did the student follow the written instructions? 1-35 points ◯

Grade for Grammar/Mechanics ◯

Writing with Sharon Watson

Dialog and Narrative Actions

STUDENT
NAME_____

Comments:

Does the dialogue show the characters reacting to their frustrating, amusing, or scary situation? 1-20 points ◯

Does the student use actions to show what characters are doing as they speak? 1-20 points ◯

Is the dialogue interesting? 1-20 points ◯

Does the dialogue show some tension or conflict? 1-20 points ◯

Did you enjoy reading the story? 1-20 points ◯

Extra credit: Is the dialogue insightful or otherwise noteworthy? 1-10 points ◯

Grade for Content ◯

Is the dialogue punctuated correctly? Does each speaker get a new paragraph? 1-25 points ◯

How are the spelling, capitalization, punctuation, sentence fragments, run-ons, and so on? 1-25 points ◯

Was the paper handed in on time? 1-25 points ◯

Did the student follow the written instructions? 1-25 points ◯

Grade for Grammar/Mechanics ◯

Writing with Sharon Watson

Fable with Moral

STUDENT
NAME_____

Comments:

Content	Points
Does the story exemplify the moral? 1-40 points	◯
Does it show some tension or conflict? 1-30 points	◯
Did you enjoy reading the fable? 1-30 points	◯
Extra credit: Is the fable insightful or otherwise noteworthy? 1-10 points	◯
Grade for Content	◯

Grammar/Mechanics	Points
Is the dialogue punctuated correctly? Does each speaker get a new paragraph? 1-25 points	◯
How are the spelling, capitalization, punctuation, sentence fragments, run-ons, and so on? 1-25 points	◯
Was the paper handed in on time? 1-25 points	◯
Did the student follow the written instructions? 1-25 points	◯
Grade for Grammar/Mechanics	◯

Writing with Sharon Watson

Fairy Tale, Tall Tale, Just So Story, or Parable

STUDENT
NAME_____

Comments:

Is there an unusual element to the story such as talking animals, magic wishes, or larger-than-life characters? 1-20 points	◯
Does the student use a clever pattern of three? 1-15 points	◯
Is it clear that the story is told by the main character or a narrator? 1-15 pts	◯
Is the point of view (through the main character or narrator) consistent? 1-15 points	◯
Is something of interest happening in the story? 1-15 points	◯
Did you enjoy reading the story? 1-20 points	◯
Extra credit: Is the story insightful or otherwise noteworthy? 1-10 points	◯
Grade for Content	◯

Is the dialogue punctuated correctly? Does each speaker get a new paragraph? 1-25 points	◯
How are the spelling, capitalization, punctuation, sentence fragments, run-ons, and so on? 1-25 points	◯
Was the paper handed in on time? 1-25 points	◯
Did the student follow the written instructions? 1-25 points	◯
Grade for Grammar/Mechanics	◯

Writing with
Sharon Watson

Made in the USA
Middletown, DE
20 March 2023

26748671R00071